The Soldiers of
Fort Mackinac

The Soldiers of Fort Mackinac

AN ILLUSTRATED HISTORY * PHIL PORTER

Mackinac State Historic Parks and Michigan State University Press

Mackinac Island and East Lansing

∞ The paper used in this publication meets the minimum requirements
of ANSI/NISO Z39.48-1992 (R 1997) (Permanence of Paper).

Michigan State University Press
East Lansing, Michigan 48823-5245

Mackinac State Historic Parks
Mackinac Island, Michigan 49757

Printed and bound in the United States.

27 26 25 24 23 22 21 20 19 18 1 2 3 4 5 6 7 8 9 10

LIBRARY OF CONGRESS CATALOGING-IN-PUBLICATION DATA
Names: Porter, Phil, 1953- author.
Title: The soldiers of Fort Mackinac : an illustrated history / Phil Porter.
Description: Mackinac Island : Mackinac State Historic Parks ;
East Lansing : Michigan State University Press, 2018. | Includes bibliographical references and index.
Identifiers: LCCN 2017025950 | ISBN 9781611862812 (cloth : alk. paper) | ISBN 9781609175610 (pdf)
Subjects: LCSH: Fort Mackinac (Mackinac Island, Mich.)—History.
| Soldiers—Michigan—Fort Mackinac (Mackinac Island)—History.
Classification: LCC F572.M16 P673 2018 | DDC 977.4–dc23 LC record available
at https://lccn.loc.gov/2017025950

Book design by Charlie Sharp, Sharp Des!gns, East Lansing, MI
Cover design by Erin Kirk New
Cover image: Fort Mackinac Rifle Team, 1886. Lieutenant Pratt is standing, third from left;
Sergeant George Robinson is standing, far left; First Sergeant Thomas Hennessy is standing, far right.

Michigan State University Press is a member of the Green Press Initiative and is committed to developing and encouraging ecologically responsible publishing practices. For more information about the Green Press Initiative and the use of recycled paper in book publishing, please visit *www.greenpressinitiative.org.*

Visit Michigan State University Press at *www.msupress.org*

For Valerie

Contents

Acknowledgments

This publication would not have been possible without the significant contribution of many individuals. I very much appreciate the advice and counsel of the following: Dr. Keith Widder, Brian Dunnigan, Julie Loehr and the staff at Michigan State University Press, Steve Brisson, Brian Jaeschke, Craig Wilson, Lynn Evans, Kathy Cryderman, Bruce Hawkins, Norman Stevens, Will Dunniway, James William Fenley, Theodore Brooke, George Mercer Brooke III, Robert Powell, Roy L. Goodale, John Griffith, Thomas St. John, Edward Nicholas, Diane Rouse, Mark Krausz, James V. Evans, Dr. William Schultz, Violet Bowling, Robert J. Fletcher, Dr. Douglas Arbittier, Thomas Shaw, Mike Savitski of Savitski Design in Ann Arbor, and Tom Hall, Curator, MacLean Collection.

Introductory Essay

More than 4,500 British and United States soldiers served at Fort Mackinac between 1780 and 1895. These soldiers constructed buildings and walls, drilled on the parade ground, marched sentry beats, and performed a myriad of maintenance and administrative duties in support of the fort's strategic military function. Beyond their military duties, Fort Mackinac soldiers also married and raised families, participated in recreational and community activities, suffered illnesses and injuries, and, upon occasion, violated army rules.

Strategically located on Mackinac Island at the juncture of Lakes Huron and Michigan, Fort Mackinac's military function changed dramatically during its 115-year history. Initially, the garrison protected and controlled the upper Great Lakes fur trade and served as an administrative center for maintaining alliances with the region's Native Americans. It was during this period that the fort saw its only combat action, when British and American forces clashed on the island during the War of 1812. By the late 1830s, the decline of the fur trade and acquisition of Indian lands that resulted in the creation of the state of Michigan diminished the fort's strategic value. It was not until after the Civil War that Fort Mackinac regained a role of importance, when it became the headquarters for the country's second national park.

British, 1781–1796

British soldiers constructed the island fort during the Revolutionary War as a more defensible alternative to Fort Michilimackinac. The position of the mainland fort, close to the water at the northern tip of Michigan's Lower Peninsula about eight miles away, provided little natural protection. By contrast, Mackinac Island's high limestone bluffs and deep, well-protected harbor offered a commanding position to repel an attack from American rebels. Even though they transferred the garrison, moved the soldiers and residents, and demolished the old fort, the function of the military at the Straits of Mackinac remained the same as it had been for decades.

Fort Mackinac was one of several late eighteenth-century British military outposts in the Great Lakes. This included forts at Oswego, Niagara, Erie, Detroit, and Mackinac. British authorities used these strategically located forts to regulate and protect the fur trade, maintain order during the summer rendezvous, and control the westward expansion of settlers. Fort commanders spent considerable time and money resolving inter-tribal conflicts, cultivating alliances through gift giving, and, during the Revolution, recruiting Native warriors to fight American rebels. It was from his new post on Mackinac Island that Lieutenant Governor

Patrick Sinclair summoned Odawa warriors from L'Arbre Croche to join a British expedition into Ohio and Kentucky that resulted in the defeat of Daniel Boone and a force of Kentucky militia at Blue Licks in August 1782.[1]

In 1783, following the American victory in the Revolution, peace negotiators from Great Britain and the United States established a new border separating Canada and the United States. As a result, several important British posts, including Oswego and Niagara on Lake Ontario, Detroit, and Fort Mackinac were now on American soil. The loss of these posts threatened to strip control of the Great Lakes fur trade from the British and destroy their fragile Indian alliances. However, the U.S. Army was severely reduced following the war and there were not enough soldiers to man these distant outposts. With the encouragement of English merchants, British soldiers retained control of these forts for 13 years after the peace treaty was signed.

Approximately 550 British soldiers served at Fort Mackinac between 1781 and 1796. Army reductions at the end of the Revolution, compounded by a potential American takeover of the fort, saw the garrison shrink to fewer than 25 men in May 1785.[2] When it became apparent that the fort would not soon be transferred to the United States, the garrison grew in strength over the next decade. The post was typically manned by 50–75 soldiers composing two companies of infantry from various regiments and a small detachment of artillerymen.

The composition of the garrison reflected the nature of the late eighteenth-century British army in North America. Most enlisted men were from the lower classes of British society and joined the army for life. During the Revolution, however, men were allowed to enlist for three-year terms or until the end of the conflict. While soldiers were poorly paid (eight pence a day, most of which was deducted for provisions, uniforms, and other services) and harshly disciplined (with corporal punishment in the form of flogging), the army did provide food, clothing, and shelter and a purpose to life. Desertion was rare and a certain esprit de corps in the form of regimental pride could be found among the troops.

Officers in the eighteenth-century British army acquired their commissions by purchase. Commissions were usually expensive and often bought by upper-class English, Scottish, and Irish gentry for their sons. There was a vast social divide between eighteenth-century British officers and enlisted men that was rarely breached. Officers congregated with the island's merchants and civic leaders and enjoyed teas, parties, and balls, while the rank and file enjoyed few diversions beyond their tightly packed barracks.

United States, 1796–1812

American soldiers, led by Major Henry Burbeck, first occupied Fort Mackinac on September 1, 1796. The signing of the Jay Treaty two years earlier resolved lingering differences between the United States and Great Britain, and enabled the peaceful transfer of the British-held posts on American soil. With troops needed to occupy the border posts, Congress reorganized the army in 1796. While the Army Act of 1796 reduced the authorized strength of the military, it confirmed the need to garrison the frontier outposts in order to establish and defend U.S. authority on its western border. In accepting the premise that the frontier posts had to be manned, Congress for the first time established a permanent, peacetime army as a cornerstone of national defense.

Fort Mackinac's first U.S. soldiers inherited a post in disrepair. Knowing that they would eventually have to relinquish the fort, British soldiers did little to improve or maintain the buildings or defensive works. Before undertaking renovations, Burbeck consulted with army leadership to ensure that the work plan would fit the strategic role of the fort. In his final instructions to Burbeck, General Anthony Wayne reminded him that the island post was "of the first consequence, being the grand depot of merchandise" for the fur trade and that it was "surrounded by the most numerous and powerful tribes of Indians in the Wilderness of the West."[3] In other words, under American control the fort would continue to serve as a strategic post for protecting and regulating the fur trade, and for developing and maintaining alliances with upper Great Lakes Indians.

In August 1797 General James Wilkinson traveled to Mackinac Island to personally review the fort's condition. This is the only time that the army's commanding officer ever visited Fort Mackinac. Wilkinson, Burbeck, and artillery officer Captain Moses Porter spent several days critically reviewing the fort's buildings, walls, earthworks, and surrounding topography. On August 19 Wilkinson rendered his decision and provided Burbeck with his plan of proposed improvements. Noting that the fort was dominated by the heights approximately 700 yards north of the post, Wilkinson declared that any attempt to make it "tenable against the attacks of artillery" would be a "useless dissipation of labour and treasure." Instead, Wilkinson directed that the fort should be rendered "impregnable to the attacks of small armys."[4] Over the next two years fort soldiers rebuilt the fort according to Wilkinson's plan. Rotted crib-style wooden walls were removed and the existing limestone ravelin became the new north wall. An additional stone wall was added west of the south sally port to reinforce the front of the work. Stone and heavy timber blockhouses were constructed in 1798 over the old British bastions along the north and east walls of the fort. The following year soldiers built an additional, smaller blockhouse along the southwest wall of the fort overlooking the town and pasture. This massive rebuilding project, completed in 1799, established the general configuration of the fort that remained throughout its occupation.

Even before the work was completed, Major General Alexander Hamilton recommended that the fort be abandoned. Arguing that the post did not "materially awe the Indians" and was "out of reach of support," Hamilton proposed moving the troops to Fort Lernoult, in Detroit.[5] General Wilkinson, now in charge of the western army and reporting directly to Hamilton, countered that Mackinac should not only be fortified but that a second fort should be built on the high ground and a garrison of 250 men assigned to Mackinac. While Hamilton refused to expand the garrison or add a new fort, he did not close the post. Rather, he split the command, sending Burbeck and the bulk of his troops to Detroit and leaving Lieutenant Richard Whiley with a small detachment of 35 infantrymen and artillerists at Mackinac.

Fort Mackinac remained a largely forgotten backwater post until President Thomas Jefferson reorganized the army in 1802. Generally suspicious of a national standing army, Jefferson reduced the size of country's armed forces and concentrated troops on the frontier and at seacoast batteries and federal arsenals. Although he shrank the army, Jefferson and Secretary of War Henry Dearborn emphasized the importance of Mackinac Island in the chain of security, communication, and transportation along the Great Lakes border. In the summer of 1802 Fort Mackinac once again became a two-company post under the command of Lieutenant Colonel Thomas Hunt, and within a year Fort Mackinac was the nation's sixth largest post with more than 120 soldiers. In May 1805 the garrison was again reduced when Lieutenant Colonel Jacob Kingsbury removed the infantry company to establish Fort Belle Fontaine near the confluence of the Mississippi and Missouri Rivers. Seven years later it became clear that a single company of artillerists was not sufficient to garrison this post on the edge of the Canadian frontier when British troops from nearby Fort St. Joseph, located forty miles northeast of Mackinac on St. Joseph's Island in the St. Mary's River, successfully attacked and captured Fort Mackinac at the outbreak of the War of 1812.

Most of the officers who served at Fort Mackinac between 1796 and 1812 had significant military experience.[6] Henry Burbeck, Thomas Hunt, Jacob Kingsbury, Moses Porter, and Abner Prior all served with the Continental Army during the American Revolution. Richard Whiley, Ebenezer Massey, James Sterrett, and John Michael participated in the Ohio Indian Wars of the 1790s. Unlike British army officers who purchased their commissions, U.S. Army officers were appointed directly by the president. There was no formal training for officers. The U.S. Military Academy at West Point did not graduate its first class until 1802, and the first West Point graduate did not arrive at Fort Mackinac until after the War of 1812. It was not uncommon for talented enlisted men to be commissioned as officers. Thomas Hunt began his career as a sergeant in Captain Craft's Company of Minutemen at Lexington and Concord in 1775, and Richard Whiley so distinguished himself in 1794 as a dragoon sergeant at the Battle of Fallen Timbers that General Anthony Wayne personally recommend him for a commission.

Francis Le Barron, Fort Mackinac's first U.S. medical officer, began his career in 1800 as a surgeon's mate in the U.S. Navy. Two years later he resigned his naval commission and was appointed garrison surgeon's mate at Fort Mackinac. After leaving Mackinac, Le Barron was promoted to surgeon in 1808 and was appointed U.S. Army apothecary general during the War of 1812. Le Barron was replaced by Dr. Sylvester Day, who remained in the army until his death in 1851 when, after 44 years in service, he was the oldest member of the medical corps.

Officers were paid commensurate with their rank. Pay was based on a monthly rate, but the fort's isolated location, especially in winter, meant that there could be long delays between paychecks. Lieutenant Colonels Thomas Hunt and Jacob Kingsbury were the highest-paid officers during this period, earning $60 per month. Major Henry Burbeck received $50 per month, while captains earned $40, first lieutenants $30, and second lieutenants $25. Interestingly, these rates remained unchanged for half a century, as it was not until 1857 that officers received a pay increase. The highest-paid enlisted men were artillery artificers, who were skilled at carpentry, masonry, boat building, and other trades and earned $10 per month. Sergeants earned $8, corporals $7, musicians $6, and privates $5.[7]

As in the British army, military discipline in the early nineteenth-century U.S. Army was quick and brutal by modern standards. The *Rules and Articles for the Government of the Armies of the United States, first approved by Congress in 1789 and amended in 1806*, provided a set of regulations governing the conduct of the country's military and naval forces. Post commanders convened garrison courts-martial to address military crimes, including absence without leave, fighting, thievery, and other violations. Drunkenness was often the root cause of many offenses. Courts could impose penalties as severe as 100 lashes on the bare back, cash fines equaling one month's pay, and incarceration for up to one month. Typical was the case of John White, who faced a garrison court on December 2, 1804. White, a private in Captain Dunham's artillery company, was tried and convicted of being intoxicated and absent from the evening parade the day before. White's punishment of 50 lashes was administered at roll call that same evening.[8]

British, 1812–1815

British soldiers, with the support of Canadian militia and Native American warriors, captured Fort Mackinac at the beginning of the War of 1812. This action was a strategic move to gain control of the most important post in the upper Great Lakes and ensure the allegiance of the region's Native Americans during the conflict. The declaration of war reached British troops at Fort St. Joseph in the spring of 1812. Here, Captain Charles Roberts gathered about 400 Odawa, Ojibway, Menominee, Winnebago, and Dakota warriors. These sympathetic Native Americans, along with 150 French-Canadian and Métis voyageurs and nearly 50 red-coated soldiers, comprised an imposing force ready to support the British cause. On July 16 Roberts's force set sail to attack Fort Mackinac.

Roberts landed his force on the north side of the island under the cover of darkness. The British force quickly moved to the high ground behind Fort Mackinac, where they aimed two six-pound cannons at "the most defenseless part of the garrison." The next morning Roberts commenced his attack by firing a warning shot from one of the six-pounders. He sent a flag of truce and summons to surrender to Lieutenant Porter Hanks, who, for the first time, learned that war had been declared. It was shortly after 10:00 a.m. on July 17, 1812. The war's first land action in U.S. territory was underway.

Lieutenant Hanks had few options. He faced an overwhelming force of 600 hostile troops poised to attack his weakest position. With a force of fewer than 60 men, Hanks surrendered without a fight in order to "prevent a general massacre." Captain Roberts took command of Fort Mackinac and confined Lieutenant Hanks and his soldiers until they could be sent on parole to the American post at Detroit.

British soldiers manned Fort Mackinac for the duration of the war. These soldiers, totaling about 350 men, came from several regiments as assigned by the commander of British forces in Canada. Soldiers from the 10th Royal Veteran Battalion, assisted by a sergeant and two gunners of the Royal Artillery, led the successful attack and capture of Fort Mackinac on July 17, 1812, and initially garrisoned the post. Hardly a crack fighting force, the Royal Veteran Battalion was composed of older, worn-out veterans, barely capable of managing basic garrison duties. When facing the prospect of defending the newly captured fort with these men, their commander, Captain Charles Roberts, described his soldiers as "so debilitated and worn down by unconquerable drunkenness that neither the fear of punishment, the love of fame or the honor of the country can animate them to extraordinary exertions."[9] Beyond their physical limitations, the company was also small. Counting fewer than 50 redcoats under his command, Roberts pleaded for additional soldiers to reinforce the island fort. With regular troops unavailable, Roberts received authority to raise a "Corps of Loyal Fencibles" to augment his command in June 1813. By the end of the summer the corps, consisting of roughly 50 soldiers and officers and known as the "Michigan Fencibles," was mustered and performed garrison duty. This was the first of several volunteer units that served at Fort Mackinac to support or replace regular army troops.

Significant American victories in the fall of 1813 turned the tide of war in favor of the United States and compelled British commanders to reinforce Fort Mackinac. Commodore Oliver Hazard Perry's victory in the Battle of Lake Erie in September 1813 wrested control of the shipping lanes supplying Detroit from the British. Major General Henry Proctor, unable to ensure the flow of supplies to his troops at Fort Detroit, abandoned the post and led his troops into southern Ontario, where they were pursued and overtaken by American soldiers under the command of Major General William Henry Harrison. Harrison's victory at the Battle of Moraviantown on the Thames River on October 5, 1813, including the death of the powerful and influential Shawnee chief Tecumseh, further strengthened American control over the region. The twin defeats at Lake Erie and Moraviantown left Fort Mackinac isolated and vulnerable to attack.

Captain Richard Bullock of the 41st Regiment of Foot took command of Fort Mackinac in September 1813. He soon learned of the British losses on the lower lakes and requested an additional 200 infantrymen and 20 artillerists to reinforce his island fort. Bullock also began strengthening his defenses while developing plans for constructing a "stockade[d] Blockhouse" on the heights overlooking Fort Mackinac.[10] Governor General George Prevost supported Bullock's request and spoke at length of the importance of preserving control over Mackinac in a letter to Henry Bathurst, British secretary of state for war and the colonies:

> Its geographical position is admirable. Its influence extends and is felt amongst the Indian tribes at New Orleans and the Pacific Ocean; vast tracts of country look to it for protection and supplies, and it gives security to the great establishments of the Northwest and Hudson's Bay Companies by supporting the Indians on the Mississippi. . . . From these observations, our Lordship will be enabled to judge how necessary the possession of this valuable post on the outskirts of these extensive provinces is becoming to their future security and protection.[11]

To reinforce Bullock, Prevost sent Lieutenant Colonel Robert McDouall of the Glengarry Light Infantry Fencibles, two companies of Royal Newfoundland Fencible Infantry, and a small detachment of artillerists to Mackinac in the spring of 1814.[12] McDouall took command of the fort on May 18 and continued reinforcing its defensive works and soon began constructing

Fort George, Bullock's longed-for post on the top of the island.

While McDouall was strengthening his defenses at Mackinac, U.S. troops in Detroit were making final preparations for an expedition north to capture the island post. Lieutenant Colonel George Croghan commanded a force including five companies of regular troops from the 17th, 19th, and 24th Regiments of Infantry, a detachment from the U.S. Corps of Artillery, Colonel William Cotgreave's Regiment of Ohio Volunteers, and some U.S. Marines. This force of approximately 750 men, transported in a naval squadron of seven ships under the command of Captain Arthur Sinclair, left Detroit on July 3.

After a three-week journey north that included a failed attempt to locate and destroy a British naval base at Nottawasaga Bay and a successful raid up the St. Mary's River, where they burned the abandoned British post at St. Joseph's Island and destroyed British fur interests at Sault Ste. Marie, the U.S. force arrived at Mackinac. On August 4 the American force landed on the north side of the island and Croghan led his troops to a small farm about a mile inland. There Croghan engaged McDouall's force, which was supported by 350 Native warriors from several upper Great Lakes Indian nations. McDouall had taken the superior position on the rising ground on the south side of the open farm field and placed his Native allies in the adjacent woods. Unable to advance by frontal assault, Croghan sent his second-in-command, Major Andrew Hunter Holmes, and a contingent of regular troops through the woods to attack the British left flank. McDouall's Menominee warriors ambushed and killed Holmes and several other American soldiers as they repelled the assault. Demoralized and realizing that his strategy was failing, Croghan ordered a retreat and returned to his ships. A subsequent naval blockade of the island was similarly unsuccessful, thereby ending the American attempt to recapture Fort Mackinac and regain control of the upper Great Lakes during the war.

On Christmas Eve 1814, American and British authorities in Ghent, Belgium, agreed to terms of peace ending the War of 1812. The Treaty of Ghent, which was ratified by the U.S. Senate in February, restored the prewar boundary between Michigan and Canada, thereby returning Mackinac Island to the United States. On July 18, 1815, U.S. soldiers peacefully returned to Mackinac Island and Lieutenant Colonel Robert McDouall reluctantly surrendered the post, "a Fortress built by nature for herself," that he had so skillfully defended.

American, 1815–1861

The role and importance of Fort Mackinac changed dramatically between 1815 and the outbreak of the Civil War. Initially a strategic post defending the country's northern border and protecting the American fur trade, the post gradually waned in significance as it approached midcentury. By the mid-1830s the fur trade was in decline. The American Fur Company declared bankruptcy in 1842 and ceased trading in 1847. As the country moved westward, soldiers that once served Fort Mackinac were needed to man new forts and fight new battles. The need to cultivate and maintain alliances with regional Indian tribes declined as British influence waned and Native lands were acquired and included in the new states of Michigan, Wisconsin, and Minnesota.

U.S. soldiers and civilian authorities faced a complex and challenging task when they arrived at Mackinac in the summer of 1815. Native Americans remained the dominant and potentially hostile population throughout the region, and British traders continued to support the tribes and actively pursue the fur trade in U.S. territories through new and refortified posts on the Canadian side of the lakes, including Fort Collier (Drummond Island, Michigan), Fort Malden (Amherstburg, Ontario), and Fort George (Niagara-on-the Lake, Ontario). The army addressed these threats by stationing the entire 5th Regiment of Infantry at Detroit and briefly headquartering the 3rd Regiment of Infantry at Fort Mackinac, which subsequently supplied soldiers to Fort Dearborn (near Chicago) and the newly constructed Fort Howard at Green Bay. This was the only time in its 115-year history that Fort Mackinac served as a regimental headquarters. In November 1816 the

Lake Nipigon
Lake of the Woods
Rainy Lake
Lake Superior
Montreal
Ottawa River
Lake Nipissing
St. Lawrence River
inset area
Lake Huron
Lake Ontario
Oswego
Fort George
Fort Niagara
Fort Erie
Green Bay
Mississippi River
Lake Michigan
Fort Malden
Detroit
Lake Erie
Chicago
Ohio River
Blue Licks
Atlantic Ocean
0
600 kilometers
0
600 miles
Lake Superior
Sault Ste. Marie
St. Joseph Island
St. Marys River
Fort Joseph
Drummond Island
Lake Michigan
St. Ignace
Mackinac Island
Fort Mackinac
Round Island
Straits of Mackinac
Lake Huron
Fort Michilimackinac
Mill Creek
Bois Blanc Island
Cheboygan R.
L'Arbre Croche
N
20 miles

garrison numbered 355 men, the largest contingent of soldiers to ever serve at Fort Mackinac.[13] This influx of soldiers necessitated construction of the wood quarters and billeting men in every available building in the fort and temporary residences in the village. American soldiers also occupied Fort George on the top of the island, now named Fort Holmes in honor of the major killed on August 4, 1814, during the Battle of Mackinac Island. The need to garrison the small post ceased by late 1817 as the likelihood of attack waned, and Fort Holmes was soon permanently abandoned.[14]

On April 29, 1816, Congress passed a law restricting the distribution of fur trade licenses on U.S. lands to American citizens. British merchants who had long-established trade networks in the upper Great Lakes were now forced to trade north of the border. This opened the door for American Fur Company owner John Jacob Astor, who purchased British supplies and buildings on American soil and established his American Fur Company with Mackinac Island as the Northern Department headquarters. Astor had actively petitioned Washington to pass the new trade bill and further demonstrated his political maneuvering by securing military assistance for his enterprise. In June 1816, Secretary of War William H. Crawford communicated the government's desire to support Astor and the American Fur Company when he ordered Fort Mackinac's post commander to "give to these gentlemen every possible facility and aid in the prosecution of their business that may be compatible with your public duties."[15]

However, just as Astor was laying the foundation for his fur empire at Mackinac, the army began shrinking the garrison at Fort Mackinac. Companies D and H, 3rd Infantry, were transferred to other Great Lakes posts in June 1820, leaving Captain Benjamin Pierce's company of artillerists as the sole caretakers of the fort. One year later Congress cut the size of the army by consolidating and eliminating regiments and reducing the number of officers. Pierce's company was cut in half and by June 1821 Fort Mackinac was manned by fewer than 60 soldiers.[16]

The reduction in troops mirrored the slowly declining military importance of Fort Mackinac. The 1816 ban on Canadian fur traders operating on American soil served to gradually break the mercantile bond and influence that British authorities exerted over their Native American allies in the upper Great Lakes. A series of land treaties beginning with the Treaty of Saginaw in 1819, and continuing through the Treaty of Washington in 1836 and the LaPointe Treaty in 1842, transferred vast portions of Indian land to the United States. These transactions diffused the tension that resulted from an influx of white settlers on Indian lands and reduced the need for military intervention. Finally, the construction of Fort Brady in Sault Ste. Marie, Michigan in 1822 meant that Fort Mackinac was no longer on the front line of defense between the United States and Canada. As a result, the army concluded that a small force of 50–100 men (one or two companies of soldiers) was more than enough to serve the military purpose of the post for the next several decades. And when the soldiers were needed elsewhere, the army did not hesitate to remove them from Mackinac.

The U.S. Army abandoned Fort Mackinac four times between 1837 and 1861. On June 10, 1837, Companies A and 2nd Infantry left the post for service in Florida as part of the U.S. Army effort during the Second Seminole War (1835–1842) in Florida. For the next three years, Ordnance Sergeant Robert G. Dunn served as caretaker of the fort. In this capacity, Dunn maintained the buildings, grounds, and ordnance stores, and represented the government in dealings with the local community. Dunn occasionally hosted traveling soldiers at the island fort, including General Winfield Scott, who conducted an inspection tour of upper Great Lakes forts in June and July 1839.[17] Two years later Scott was appointed commanding general of the U.S. Army, a position he held until 1861. Shortly after Scott left Mackinac, the post was briefly occupied by a single company of artillerists, but the fort was not fully regarrisoned until May 1840.

Federal forces also vacated Fort Mackinac during the last year of the Mexican-American War (1846–1848). Soldiers of Company C, 2nd Infantry, under the command of Captain Silas Casey, left the island post on May 10, 1847, and arrived at Camp Perote, Veracruz, Mexico, on June 30. The fort was briefly garrisoned by the soldiers of Company G, 15th Infantry before they, too, were shipped off to Mexico in June 1847. For the duration of the war the post was under the care of Captain Morgan Gage and his company of Michigan Volunteers (Brady's Guard).

Tension between white settlers and Seminole Indians once again erupted into conflict in southern Florida in the mid-1850s. On October 12, 1856, Captain Thomas Williams and Company L, 4th Artillery, vacated Fort Mackinac bound for Fort Myers, Florida. Ordnance Sergeant William Marshall was the sole custodian of the fort for the next two years, except during the summer of 1857, when Company E, 2nd Artillery, briefly occupied the post. Marshall, who arrived at the fort in 1848, continued to serve at the island post until his death in 1884, making him Fort Mackinac's longest-serving soldier. At the outbreak of the Civil War, it was Marshall who once again remained behind to care for the fort when Captain Henry Pratt and Company G, 2nd Artillery, left the post in the spring of 1861 to support the Union army's defense of Washington, DC.[18]

More than 2,100 soldiers served at Fort Mackinac between 1815 and 1861. This included 145 regular army officers. Sixty were graduates of the U.S. Military Academy at West Point, New York. The rest were appointed directly from civilian life, including the 17 medical officers who served the post during this period. The majority of officers (57 percent) were from the mid-Atlantic states, primarily New York, Virginia, and Pennsylvania, followed by New England (28 percent), and the Midwest (11 percent). Four officers hailed from southern states and three were foreign born, all from Ireland.[19] Nearly every Fort Mackinac officer had wartime experience, either before or after they served at Mackinac. Fifty were veterans of the War of 1812, a like number participated in the Mexican War, and 28 saw action during the Seminole or 1832 Black Hawk wars. Forty-six officers served in either regular or volunteer units during the Civil War, including seven who resigned their commissions in the U.S. Army and donned the gray uniforms of the Confederacy. Brevet Brigadier General George Mercer Brooke was the fort's highest-ranking officer when he commanded the post in 1832, but 24 others rose to the rank of general after their service at Fort Mackinac, most during the Civil War.

Pay progressed slowly for officers during this period. In 1815 a captain was paid $60 per month, given five daily rations for himself and his family, and allotted two servants. Forty-six years later, as he departed for service in the Civil War, his pay was only $20 higher per month, with no additional rations or servants.[20] Similarly, a first lieutenant's pay was raised from $30 to $50, while a second lieutenant's pay increased from $25 to $45. Promotions provided one avenue to a larger salary for officers, but, with the exception of the Mexican War, the army remained relatively small and the opportunities for advancement were limited. After briefly serving as temporary commander of Fort Mackinac in the summer of 1841, Lieutenant John Phelps grumbled that it would be a long time before he would again experience such authority. In writing to his sister he lamented, "I feel that anything worthy of my notice at all is beyond my reach, and so I live like the boy waiting till time shall make him a man. I have not much hope that it will ever make a colonel of me."[21]

The vast majority of enlisted men during this period were drawn from the country's lower socioeconomic classes, for whom the prospect of basic food and shelter outweighed the meager pay, severe discipline, danger, and boredom that accompanied military life. Pay increases to enlisted men during this period were also few and far between, just slightly outpacing the raises received by commissioned officers. After a slight boost during the War of 1812, enlisted men's monthly pay returned to prewar levels that had been in place since 1798. Sergeants earned $8 per month, corporals $7, musicians $6, and privates $5. Pay was increased just three times over the next 45 years, and by 1861 sergeants received $17 per month, corporals $13, musicians $12, and privates $11.[22] While the salary was less than that of common laborers, the soldier was also assured of housing and daily rations.[23]

Nevertheless, the army was an attractive option for the growing number of immigrants streaming into the country during this period. The percentage of foreign-born soldiers steadily increased as the tide of immigration grew from 151,000 in the 1820s to 2,314,000 in the 1850s.[24] This pattern held true at Fort Mackinac. In 1829 only 24 percent of the soldiers in Captain Robert McCabe's company of the 5th Infantry were foreign born, five from Ireland, three from England, and one each from Canada and Germany. By contrast, immigrants comprised 64 percent of Captain Henry Pratt's artillery company in 1860. Reflecting changing immigration patterns, Pratt's company included 15 soldiers from Germany, nine from Ireland, three from Canada, two each from Italy and England, and one each from Scotland, Denmark, and France.[25] The growing number of foreign-born recruits created an increasingly diverse and sometimes volatile mixture of cultures and languages. Communication, especially with non-English-speaking soldiers, provided numerous challenges for officers. The army provided no formal opportunity to learn English, and soldiers were sometimes slow to adopt the national tongue. When Wolf Grenner, a German-born private in the 4th Artillery, faced charges of deserting Fort Mackinac in 1851, he needed an interpreter to assist him at his general court-martial, even though he'd been in the army for more than five years.[26]

The maintenance and care of the post was a constant challenge for Fort Mackinac's officers and enlisted men during this period. Inspectors often complained about the dilapidated condition of the post, prompting frequent repairs, additions, and improvements. By 1861 the fort had been substantially rebuilt and only the exterior stone walls, blockhouses, officer's stone quarters, and powder magazine remained from the pre–War of 1812 fort. The officer's wood quarters (1816) was the first addition, built to help accommodate the large number of troops assigned to the post after the war. Little was done to improve or repair the fort over the next decade, and by 1826 the post was barely habitable. The July 14 report to the inspector general described the fort as being "too nearly in ruin to afford any longer either comfortable or safe quarters for the garrison." Despite a recommendation that repairs would be "but an idle waste of time and money," the army resolved to renovate the post.[27] Over the next two years post commandant Major Alexander Ramsay Thompson supervised the most significant construction project since the fort was built fifty years earlier. New buildings included a post hospital that was built and burned to the ground in 1827, then rebuilt a year later. The soldiers' barracks, guardhouse, and blacksmith shop were replaced with new structures, and a bakehouse, carpenter shop, and ordnance storehouse were combined into a single new structure on the east end of the parade ground. Other new structures added during this period include the officers' hill quarters (1835) and a new, two-story hospital (1860). The 1828 soldiers' barracks was destroyed by fire and rebuilt in 1855, and consumed by fire again three years later along with the blacksmith shop, and the row of buildings on the east end of the parade ground. Replacement structures, including a two-story barracks, blacksmith shop, bakehouse, quartermaster's storehouse, and post headquarters, were all constructed over the next three years. [28]

When not involved in construction projects soldiers kept busy standing guard, practicing military drills, policing the grounds, conducting maintenance projects, cutting and storing firewood, and addressing other duties needed to maintain the post. The soldier's daily routine was often tedious and dull, especially during the winter. Boredom, frustration, personal conflicts, and other symptoms of dissatisfaction, often fueled by alcohol, occasionally led to soldierly misbehavior.

As in earlier periods, Fort Mackinac officers used garrison courts to adjudicate minor crimes. Hundreds of cases were tried at Fort Mackinac between 1815 and 1861. The typical problems—desertion, absence without leave, neglect of duty, disorderly conduct, and drunkenness on duty—remained the same through the period. Penalties, limited to one-month sentences, typically included incarceration and reduction in rank or elimination of pay. While flogging was abandoned as a form of punishment between 1812 and 1833, officers often resorted to other creative and sometimes brutal forms of physical punishment.

A series of cases in the fall of 1844 illustrate the typical crimes and variety of punishments during this period. On September 14 Private George Thompson was charged with being in "contempt of authority" for going into the village of Mackinac Island without permission. The three-officer court led by Captain Moses Merrill found Thompson guilty and fined him $4. The same court charged Private George Miles with drunkenness on duty. Miles was convicted and, as a result of being a habitual offender, fined $5 and required to wear a neck yoke weighing four pounds for 30 days, and a ball and chain for the same period of time. Two months later, Private Miles once again found himself facing charges in a garrison court-martial led by Captain Merrill. Miles was found guilty of being absent without leave and sentenced to "carry on his back, ten six-pound shot, every alternate two hours for fifteen days and nights; when not carrying shot to be kept in light prison [as compared to the black hole] and to be kept in solitary confinement on bread and water for fifteen days." The same court found Private Andrew O'Connor guilty of disobedience of orders when he refused to report to police duty. The court convicted O'Connor but remitted his sentence of five days' hard labor in charge of the guard because it was his first offense.[29]

Fort Mackinac commanders convened general courts-martial to deal with serious breaches of military conduct. General courts required a minimum of five officers and could levy sentences lasting longer than 30 days, discharge soldiers from service, and impose corporal punishments. Flogging, which had been abandoned as a form of punishment by the army in 1812, was reinstated between 1833 and 1861 for the sole crime of desertion. The court's sentences were not final until approved by departmental commanders or, in the case of an officer, by the president of the United States.

Thirty-six enlisted men faced general courts-martial at Fort Mackinac between 1830 and 1861. The most common crimes were desertion, neglect of duty, and mutiny—alcohol was often a contributing factor. Major William Hoffman, 6th Regiment of Infantry, traveled to Mackinac Island in the late summer of 1860 to preside over a general court that tried several cases, including charges of desertion against Privates Charles Benedict and William Henderson. Each was found guilty and sentenced to forfeit his pay, be flogged, and "indelibly marked with a 'D' 1½ inches long" under his left arm, and be drummed out of the service. Despite their sentence, the court recommended leniency for Benedict "in consideration of his youth . . . he being but a recruit at the time of his desertion." Department commander Major General John Wool accepted the recommendation of the court and remitted all of Benedict's sentence except for the loss of pay. Henderson, however, was afforded no relief and received "50 lashes on the bare back well laid on with a raw hide" before being drummed out of the fort.[30]

Thirty years earlier, eight soldiers charged with mutiny stood before a general court in one of the most dramatic and infamous incidents in Fort Mackinac's 115-year history. On Christmas Day 1829, Private Charles Eddo led a group of armed soldiers onto the parade ground to rescue Private Levi Stephens, who was being flogged by Lieutenant Ephraim Kirby Smith for bringing liquor into the fort. Smith had a long history of savagely disciplining soldiers without the benefit of trials and using methods that were clearly abusive and contrary to the standards of military discipline. Eddo himself had been both flogged and caned by Smith within months prior to the mutiny for minor infractions. Intoxicated from a long day of drinking Christmas toasts, Eddo and his fellow mutineers, armed with muskets fixed with bayonets, clashed with Smith on the parade ground. Although no shots were fired, Smith received minor wounds on his hand and shoulder, and broke his sword slashing at and slightly wounding Private Henry Gretzler. As Smith retreated, Lieutenants Isaac Lynde and Caleb Sibley arrived and, with the assistance of soldiers on guard duty, quelled the rebellion. The offending soldiers were identified, arrested, and placed in the post guardhouse. Not satisfied to wait for a trial, Lieutenant Smith ordered Genury, Gretzler, and Urquardt to his quarters where he personally flogged them with a cowhide whip.[31]

Lieutenant Colonel Enos Cutler, who was dining in town with two other senior officers during the mutiny, convened a general court-martial on May 13, 1830. Seven soldiers were convicted of mutiny and one was acquitted. Privates Eddo, Francis, Genury, Gretzler, Shearer, and Urquardt were sentenced to perform hard labor wearing a ball and chain for the remainder of their enlistment, to be kept in confinement when not at labor, forfeit four-fifths of their pay, and have their heads shaved and be drummed out of the army at the end of their enlistment. Private Peter White received the lesser sentence of six months of hard labor and police duty, loss of pay and whiskey rations for six months, and confinement in the black hole when not at labor. In reviewing the case, General Winfield Scott remitted the sentences of Genury, Gretzler, and Urquardt because of the flogging "illegally inflicted" on them by Smith. Four months later, at the recommendation of Cutler and in recognition of Smith's inappropriate conduct, Scott remitted the remainder of the sentences for Eddo and Francis.[32]

Lieutenant Smith's brutal behavior did not escape the notice of his superiors. Charged with "Illegal, Arbitrary and Unmilitary Conduct," Smith was brought before a general court-martial convened by Lieutenant Colonel Cutler at Fort Mackinac on August 9, 1830. Several witnesses, including officers, enlisted men, and Post Surgeon Richard Satterlee, provided detailed testimony to six separate acts of illegally flogging or beating soldiers. Despite a rambling, seventeen-page defense, Smith was convicted and dismissed from the army. The sentence was approved by President Andrew Jackson, who stated that an "Officer who inflicts corporal punishment whilst in the heat of passion . . . renders himself doubly obnoxious to the charge of arbitrary conduct." Smith was dismissed from service on October 1.[33] Eighteen months later, through the influence of family and political allies, President Jackson restored Smith's commission in the army.

American, 1861–1895

Fort Mackinac experienced significant change between the outbreak of the Civil War and the closing of the post in 1895. With the exception of a few months in the summer of 1862, the fort was essentially abandoned during the war. Even after the war, the island post was initially manned by temporary reserve units and disabled veterans, a testimony to its lack of strategic value. In 1875, however, the fort received new life when it became the administrative headquarters for Mackinac National Park. A second company was assigned to the post, the facilities were expanded and modernized, and Fort Mackinac became a desirable and popular station for late nineteenth-century U.S. soldiers.

On April 28, 1861, just 16 days after the Confederate bombardment of Fort Sumter, Captain Henry Pratt abandoned the post and set sail from Mackinac Island with his company of artillerymen to support the Union cause. Sixty-one-year-old Ordnance Sergeant William Marshall once again remained behind to care for the fort. During the next six years Marshall dutifully maintained the military buildings, cared for the cannons and ordnance equipment, and filed a myriad of reports with military officials. Only twice during this period were other soldiers assigned to the fort, most notably during the summer of 1862, when the post was used to incarcerate Confederate political prisoners.

In April 1862 Union General Andrew Johnson, Tennessee's military governor, arrested Washington Barrow, Josephus Conn Guild, and William G. Harding. All three men were wealthy and influential residents of Tennessee, where they actively supported the Confederacy. Johnson charged the men with "treasonous inclinations" and refusing to pledge an oath of loyalty to the United States. Because they had no military status, the men became state or "political" prisoners. Johnson simply wanted them removed from Tennessee so that they could not support the Confederacy.[34]

Johnson sent the prisoners to Detroit, but Secretary of War Edwin Stanton indicated that they would eventually be incarcerated at Fort Mackinac. The Confederates remained in Detroit while Stanton authorized an independent company of Michigan volunteers for the sole purpose of guarding the prisoners. Grover Salmon Wormer became company captain, and he recruited most of the soldiers at his Masonic Hall office on Detroit's Jefferson Avenue. Wormer mustered his 50-man unit—the "Stanton Guard"—into service on May 10,

1861, and set sail for Mackinac Island with his prisoners on board the steamer *Illinois* four days later.

Sergeant Marshall provided Fort Mackinac quarters for Wormer's men, and the prisoners were assigned to the officers' wood quarters. The prisoners were lightly guarded and generally treated with respect and dignity. They were free to roam the fort during daylight hours and confined to quarters only at night. Additionally, Wormer gave them permission to visit the village and stroll the island under a three-man guard for up to three hours a day. Despite the many indulgences they received, the Confederate prisoners chafed at their incarceration. They missed their families, tired of the ever-present guards, and longed to return home.

By midsummer the prisoners began considering the unpleasant prospect of spending the winter at Mackinac. On August 1, 1862, Guild swore allegiance to the United States and Harding signed his oath a few days later. Both men left Mackinac Island in September. Barrow refused to sign, and the army transferred him to Johnson's Island Military Prison near Sandusky, Ohio. Once the prisoners were gone from Mackinac, the Stanton Guard was no longer needed. The army disbanded the unit and encouraged the men to enlist in Michigan volunteer units. Captain Wormer and his men left the island post on September 30, 1862.[35] As autumn's cool winds began to sweep across the Straits of Mackinac, Ordnance Sergeant Marshall remained behind as the sole defender of the fort, a post that he faithfully manned for the duration of the war.

The War Department mustered out over one million volunteers at the end of the Civil War. The regular army, which contained only 22,000 soldiers by the time Lee surrendered at Appomattox Court House in the spring of 1865, was soon expanded to meet the country's military needs. Initially increased to 57,000 soldiers in 1867, the authorized force was reduced by Congress to 45,000 two years later, and to 27,000 in 1876. The army was not expanded until the Spanish-American War in the late 1890s.[36]

The primary function of the postwar army was to enforce the policies of Reconstruction in the South and support the country's relentless western expansion through Indian lands. Manning Fort Mackinac remained a low priority, and the army was more than happy to leave Sergeant Marshall in charge of the post for more than a year after the war ended. Even when the fort was regarrisoned in 1866, the army expressed its opinion of Mackinac's military importance by sending disabled war veterans. Initially, this consisted of the 4th Independent Company, Veteran Reserve Corps during the summer of 1866, followed by Company B, 43rd Regiment of Infantry the following year. When invalid units were eliminated in the 1869 reduction, the army sent Captain Leslie Smith and Company F, 1st Regiment of Infantry, to occupy the fort. This was the first of 10 regular army companies that would garrison the fort until it closed in 1895.[37]

The return of regular troops to Fort Mackinac was accompanied by a steadily growing crowd of summer visitors. Following the Civil War, Mackinac Island became an increasingly popular vacation destination as the regional economy shifted from the processing of natural resources—furs and fish—to summer tourism. In recognition of the island's growing popularity, and in an effort to preserve its natural and historic character, the federal government created Mackinac National Park in 1875. The country's second national park, Mackinac Island provided visitors with a delightful combination of natural beauty and historic charm, along with the advantage of being a healthy retreat for hay fever sufferers.

Mackinac National Park brought new life to Fort Mackinac. The park was placed under the jurisdiction of the War Department, and Secretary of War William Belknap appointed fort commander Major Alfred L. Hough park superintendent. Post commandants were given a new list of responsibilities beyond managing the fort and garrison, including enforcing park rules and regulations, cutting new roads and trails, and leasing property for cottage construction. The army added a second company of soldiers to Fort Mackinac beginning in 1876 to assist the commandant with these new tasks. The fort remained a two-company post until 1895 except in 1876–1877, when Company E, 22nd Infantry, was temporarily transferred to Fort Abraham Lincoln during the Great Sioux War and then to Pennsylvania to assist in the suppression of labor disturbances associated with the Great Railroad Strike of 1877. With the creation of Mackinac National Park, the island post was no longer just a place to store soldiers. While it did little to protect national security, Fort Mackinac did have a new pride of purpose, something that had been missing since the decline of the island fur trade in the mid-1830s.[38]

The influx of additional soldiers, as well as an overall need to modernize the fort, set off a flurry of new construction over the next 15 years that significantly expanded and improved the post. Two elegant new officers' quarters were constructed on the bluff just west of the fort in 1876. The single family dwelling became the commandant's home and the duplex next door housed the post surgeon and a company commander. The following year the sergeants' quarters duplex was constructed on the rear parade ground outside the fort. Occupied primarily by departmental staff noncommissioned officers, the building was expanded to include a third apartment in 1885 when John Fletcher, Mackinac's first quartermaster sergeant, was assigned to the fort. The new laundress quarters, constructed in 1877 next to the sergeants' quarters, provided housing for married enlisted men and their families. Ten years later the steward's quarters was built next to the post hospital to accommodate Hospital Corps staff.[39]

At the same time that the army constructed new quarters, it also made significant improvements to older residences. The officers' hill quarters was expanded and remodeled in 1874–1875. A few years later the soldiers' barracks was enlarged and the second-floor chapel converted into a squad room to accommodate the second company of soldiers. Barracks remodeling continued into the 1880s, when the army replaced rotting plaster with beaded Norway pine boards, improved air flow and ventilation, and rebuilt the imposing, columned front porch.[40]

Along with new and improved housing, the army built several support structures at Fort Mackinac during this period. A brick powder magazine constructed north of the fort enabled soldiers to move their gunpowder from the east blockhouse, which was dangerously close to several buildings, including the hospital. The old stone magazine, long abandoned and badly deteriorated, was demolished and replaced by a spacious commissary for food storage in 1878. The following year a reading room was constructed to provide educational opportunities for soldiers and their children. Several buildings, including a coal shed, scale house, and morgue were constructed in the open ground east of the fort, while a new blacksmith shop was built near the garden in front of the fort.

In marked contrast to the fort's earlier years of occupation, the army undertook projects designed to improve soldiers' morale and provide recreational opportunities. These projects were part of a broader attempt to improve army life for enlisted men beginning in the 1880s. Known as the Army Reform Movement, these measures instituted better training procedures, improved uniforms and living conditions, and provided recreational opportunities. General William T. Sherman captured the sentiment that led to reforms when, in 1883, he instructed his fellow officers, "We must now treat the soldier as a fellow-man."[41]

The War Department officially approved the construction and use of canteens for the entertainment, recreation, and amusement of enlisted men at military posts in 1889. Officers at Fort Mackinac quickly took advantage of the new policy and remodeled the wood quarters into the post canteen at a cost of $82.53. Opened on November 7, 1889, the canteen provided the men with two billiard rooms and a bar with a lunch counter. The rooms were furnished with books, magazines, and board games including backgammon, checkers, dominoes, and chess. The walls were decorated with large, framed pictures, including seven large Civil War battle scenes donated by West Bluff summer cottager Henry Leman. In the lunchroom soldiers enjoyed ham-and-cheese sandwiches with imported Swiss cheese and French mustard, light wines, and beer, including Schlitz of Milwaukee, which was sold for "five-cents per glass—large size." Beer was the main source of profit, while coffee was discontinued after three weeks for lack of interest. The canteen was immensely popular with the soldiers and enthusiastically supported by the officers, who noticed an immediate improvement in morale and behavior. Six weeks after the canteen opened, Captain Greenleaf A. Goodale proudly reported, "It is proving the greatest conservator of discipline that I have ever seen."[42]

New construction was accompanied by technological innovations that significantly improved the quality of life as compared to earlier generations of Fort Mackinac soldiers. Living conditions in the barracks squad rooms improved in the early 1870s when old wood-burning heaters and double-deck wooden bunks were replaced by coal stoves and single, iron-framed beds. The men continued to sleep on straw mattresses and wooden slats until 1885, when the army supplied them with wire spring bunk bottoms and five-inch-thick, cotton-stuffed mattresses. Post surgeon Dr. John Bailey was so impressed with the new bedding that he remarked, "Such accommodations are very much better than those furnished by ordinary hotels and may be said to be truly luxurious. They are conducive to sweet repose, comfort, cleanliness, contentment and health."[43]

Water supply to the fort improved dramatically in 1881 when a new water-pumping and storage system was installed. Using a coal-powered hot-air engine, fresh water was pumped from a spring below the fort to a 65-barrel reservoir constructed on the second floor of the North Blockhouse. From here water flowed through one-inch pipes to several fort buildings, including the post bathhouse, which was constructed "in a hygiene fever" during the fall of 1885. Dr. Bailey described the new building as "the most useful at the post." It featured six cast-iron bathtubs and hot and cold running water. The soldiers, Bailey boasted, "bathe once a week, or more, and their habits are generally cleanly."[44] Four years later plumbing contractors Sproul and McGurrin of Grand Rapids installed the fort's first water closets and flush toilets. Post commander Goodale gave his soldiers detailed instructions to use only "soft paper" and avoid throwing matches, toothpicks, and cigar stumps in the privy bowls. Violators, he warned, would be court-martialed and made to use the old privies.[45]

The addition of telegraphy improved communications at Fort Mackinac beginning in July 1883. An underwater wire from St. Ignace ran to a single station in the island village operated by Miss Maggie Donnelly. A line ran from her office to Fort Mackinac so that officers could take advantage of this technology for communicating with the outside world. As a result, written correspondence from division headquarters in New York City that required seven to 27 days of travel time by mail in the 1870s was replaced by instantaneous telegraphic service. Although most correspondence continued via mail, telegraphic communication proved very helpful in certain situations. Such was the case when Lieutenant George B. Davis provided timely communication to Lieutenant Lea Febiger, who was ordered to travel from Fort Brady to serve on a garrison court at Fort Mackinac. The almost daily telegraphic communication over the course of five days in March 1889 allowed Febiger to avoid crossing to the island on "unsafe ice."[46]

Soldiers relished service at Fort Mackinac during the National Park period. The garrison was at peace, there was little fear of attack, fatigue duty was light, and social and recreational opportunities abounded. No longer a lonely post on the nation's frontier, Mackinac Island was now a popular summer resort with plenty of diversions for off-duty soldiers. Free time allowed soldiers to stroll on park trails, dine and dance at the new hotels, picnic on nearby Round Island, and go skating and sledding in the winter. Baseball was the sporting rage of the period, and soldiers played with enthusiasm. In 1885 Lieutenant Edward Pratt, whose father and grandfather had both served at the island fort, helped organize the first Fort Mackinac baseball club in his spare time. Pratt even donated $4 to help pay for bats, balls, a catcher's mask, and flannel suits complete with elastic fittings.[47]

The starting pay for Fort Mackinac enlisted men during this period was between $13 and $34 per month, close to the wage scale prior to the Civil War. First-year privates earned $13 per month, corporals $15, duty sergeants $17, and first sergeants $22. The quartermaster sergeant was paid $23 per month, hospital stewards between $20 and $30, and ordnance and commissary sergeants $34.[48] From this pay the government deducted 12½ cents from each soldier to support the Soldiers Home, a military veteran's retirement home established in 1851. The post commandant also subtracted a sum from each soldier as set by a council of administration, usually between 50 cents and $1 per month, to pay the post laundresses.

Pay rates were higher during the Civil War, when the scale began at $16 a month for privates. When Congress reduced the scale to prewar levels in 1871, the rank and file expressed their opinions in a desertion rate that soared from 9.4 percent to 32.6 percent.[49] The reaction at Fort Mackinac was not quite so dramatic, but during the summer of 1871 Captain Leslie Smith lost nine men to desertion, about 16 percent of the enlisted population. In response to rampant desertions, Congress enacted legislation in May 1872 to improve soldiers' compensation. Base pay rates were not raised, but the new law provided for annual increases of $1 dollar per month beginning in the third year of a soldier's first enlistment. Soldiers also received a bonus for reenlistment. The private who began his army career at $13 a month now earned $16 a month by the end of his first enlistment and began his second enlistment at $18 per month. The pay for noncommissioned officers and departmental staff was raised accordingly and, along with private's pay, remained essentially unchanged until 1898.[50] Soldiers appreciated the pay raise but chafed at the provision that all income above the base pay would be retained by the government until the soldier received an honorable discharge. Retained pay, the army reasoned, rewarded the faithful soldier and discouraged the would-be deserter. Soldiers at Fort Mackinac took a different view, and Captain Smith lost an additional 14 men to desertion in 1872. "This command is so much reduced by desertions," Smith complained on July first, "that there are absolutely not men enough to perform the guard duty of one post. I have only seven privates for guard duty this morning."[51] The flow of desertions was not stemmed until the financial Panic of 1873, when jobs were hard to find and army enlistments increased.

For those who deserted and committed other military crimes, the army continued to administer discipline through garrison and general courts-martial, but with significantly less brutal methods. The army prohibited flogging beginning in 1861, and other forms of physical punishment, including carrying knapsacks loaded with cannon balls, were no longer administered by the mid-1870s.

Fort Mackinac officers convened hundreds of garrison courts-martial during this period, with 309 alone between 1884 and 1890. Garrison courts could impose maximum penalties of a one-month incarceration in the guardhouse combined with hard labor and/or loss of one month's pay. While noncommissioned officers were usually spared jail time and cash fines, they almost always lost the pay and benefits of their rank as they were reduced to privates. With no other means of discipline at their disposal, officers used garrison courts-martial to deal with nearly every minor breech of conduct at Fort Mackinac.

The crimes remained the same as they had been throughout the fort's history—absence without leave, disorderly conduct, neglect of duty, and fighting—often as a result of excessive alcohol. Typical were the cases of privates Louis Sieber and John Baseler, who faced a garrison court on February 27, 1886. Sieber was convicted of being "drunken and disorderly in the company mess room during supper" on February 23 and using "abusive and insubordinate language" to Sergeant George Robinson while being escorted to the post guardhouse. He was sentenced to forfeit one month's pay and confined at hard labor in charge of the guard for 30 days. Baseler was convicted of being "so much under the influence of intoxicating liquors as to be unable to perform his duties" while working as a teamster and disobeying orders by taking the company horse and sleigh to the village rather than to the stable as ordered. Baseler was acquitted of the drunkenness charge but found guilty of disobeying orders and sentenced to a $10 fine.[52]

Seventy-two Fort Mackinac soldiers faced general courts-martial between 1867 and 1895. These soldiers faced more serious charges such as desertion and assault and battery, and many had long histories of misbehavior. Sentences included dishonorable discharge, long-term confinement in a military penitentiary, and severe cash fines. Two cases tried on May 29, 1888, are good examples of the types of crimes and punishments associated with general courts-martial at Fort Mackinac during this period.

On the morning of May 7, 1888, at 9:00 a.m., the soldiers of Fort Mackinac queued up in front of the post headquarters, where they received their pay for the previous two months. Later that day, a group of enlisted men walked to the village to spend some of their hard-earned money in Truscott's Saloon. There, Private Thomas Conroy and Corporal William Williams engaged in a verbal argument that soon led to exchanging punches and wrestling on the floor, with Williams eventually gaining the upper hand. Later that evening, Conroy attacked Williams who was asleep in his bed in the second-floor bunk room of the soldiers' barracks. Conroy struck Williams on the head with a heavy club and was preparing to strike again when he was restrained by other soldiers. Conroy was arrested and Williams was taken, unconscious, to the post hospital, where he spent the next week recovering. Williams ultimately suffered permanent hearing loss in his left ear. Conroy was charged with "conduct to the prejudice of good order and military discipline," and found guilty by general court-martial on May 29. The twenty-two-year-old private was sentenced to forfeit his pay, and was dishonorably discharged and sentenced to be confined at hard labor for one year in the military prison at Fort Leavenworth, Kansas.[53]

On the same payday, Private Frank Darlington was reported absent without leave from fatigue duty within minutes of receiving his money. With his pockets full of cash, Darlington met local boatman Alex Lalone at British Landing and sailed to St. Ignace, where, by his own admission, he spent the night in a "house of ill fame." Darlington returned to the island the following day and hid in the woods below Plank's Grand Hotel until late afternoon, when he was arrested in the village by Sergeant Englehard Endres, taken to the post guardhouse, and eventually charged with desertion. With the help of private attorney P. M. Packard, Darlington was able to get the charge reduced from "desertion" to the lesser crime of "absence without leave," and was sentenced to be confined at hard labor at Fort Mackinac for two months.[54]

Darlington, however, was a repeat offender and found himself back in the guardhouse in October 1888 as a result of a garrison court-martial. While incarcerated, Darlington smuggled liquor—Duffy's Malt Whiskey—into the guardhouse via a rubber hose through one of the barred windows. Darlington soon found himself facing another general court-martial for his misbehavior. Without attorney Packard to help plead his case, Darlington was convicted and, like Conroy, lost his pay and was dishonorably discharged and sent to the military prison at Fort Leavenworth for a year.[55] It was here that the sad story of Private Darlington came to an end as he died of double pneumonia in April 1889.

Darlington and Conroy were just two of the more than 1,000 soldiers garrisoned at Fort Mackinac between 1867 and 1895. Reflecting the country's changing demographic and immigration patterns, the fort's enlisted men hailed from twenty-two different countries and thirty-three different states and the District of Columbia. The percentage of foreign-born soldiers in the U.S. Army steadily declined during the second half of the nineteenth century. This held true at Fort Mackinac, where the immigrant population of the fort declined from a high of 64 percent in 1860, to 51 percent, between 1867 and 1879, and eventually dwindled to 32 percent in the early 1890s. Reflecting general immigration patterns, the largest number of foreign-born soldiers in the army came from Ireland and Germany. Again, the pattern held true at Fort Mackinac, where Irishmen (42 percent) and Germans (26 percent) dominated the foreign-born population. But, as compared to the fort's earlier occupation, the garrison reflected broadening immigration patterns. Truly a cosmopolitan community during this period, Fort Mackinac soldiers also came from Canada, England, Scotland, Wales, Switzerland, Italy, France, Holland, Denmark, Norway, Sweden, Poland, Prussia, Austria, Bohemia, Russia, Greece, Turkey, and Australia.[56]

U.S.-born soldiers came primarily from northern states from the East Coast to the Mississippi River, clearly a result of the location of permanent recruiting stations. New York and Pennsylvania supplied the most soldiers, but Midwestern states, particularly Ohio and Michigan, sent an increasing number of soldiers to the fort in later years. Soldiers came to the fort from every state east of the Mississippi River (except Mississippi) as well as Minnesota, Iowa, Missouri, Arkansas, Nebraska, Kansas, and Texas.[57]

Forty-four commissioned officers served at Fort Mackinac during the period 1867 to 1895. These men served by virtue of a presidential commission received through civilian appointment, graduation from the U.S. Military Academy at West Point, promotion from the enlisted ranks, or commissions from Civil War state volunteer units. Civil War veterans dominated the officer corps for many years after the rebellion. Thirty-three of the 44 officers (75 percent) who served at Fort Mackinac during the period 1867–1895 were Civil War veterans. This group included regular army officers who remained in service after the war and volunteers who mustered out of their militia units at the end of the war and rejoined by appointment in the late 1860s.

In the 1880s U.S. Military Academy graduates began to replace the Civil War veterans who previously dominated the Fort Mackinac officer corps. While there were only two West Pointers at Fort Mackinac in the first decade after the Civil War, nine served at the island post during its last ten years. Slowly the army's officer corps was shifting from those who had brief, but intense, combat experience during the war to those who had excellent academic training but little field experience. As a result, companies often had officers with widely varying backgrounds. Captain Jacob H. Smith, a sixty-year-old Ohio-born veteran, wounded at the Battle of Shiloh in 1862 and promoted for gallant and meritorious service during the war, commanded Company D, 19th Infantry, when they arrived on the island in 1890. His staff included three West Pointers, none of whom had fought in the Civil War. The youngest, twenty-two-year-old Second Lieutenant Henry Grant Learned, was just out of the academy.[58]

Unlike enlisted men, commissioned officers enjoyed a significant pay raise as compared to their pre–Civil War salaries. In 1857 a private soldier earned $11 a month. In 1872 it was raised by 18 percent to $13, with a $1 monthly raise beginning in his third year. By contrast, a second lieutenant who earned $45 a month in 1857 received a 115 percent pay raise to $116 in 1870. Correspondingly, first lieutenants received $125, captains $150, and majors $208. However, these salaries remained unchanged from 1870 to 1898, and the only raise an officer at Fort Mackinac could look forward to was his "fogy," a 10 percent longevity pay increase given every five years.[59]

Twelve medical officers served at Fort Mackinac between 1867 and 1895. Most were commissioned officers serving as captains or lieutenants with the rank of assistant surgeon. Five were medical officers during the Civil War, where they received valuable, if harrowing, experience in field hospitals. Typical of these veterans was Dr. William Notson, who spent three years with the Union army bandaging bullet wounds, amputating limbs, and combating diseases including dysentery, typhoid fever, and malaria. Several received formal training at some of the finest medical schools in the country. Dr. Edwin Gardner, who enlisted as a private at the end of the Civil War, graduated from Harvard Medical School in 1875. Dr. William Corbusier studied medicine in California, served as surgeon in charge of the 6th Illinois Cavalry during the war, and completed his medical studies at Bellevue Hospital Medical College in New York City in 1867.[60]

When army physicians were unavailable, the medical department hired private citizens to serve the fort's medical needs. Mackinac Island physicians Drs. John R. Bailey and Hiram Mills worked as "acting assistant surgeons" during this period. While Mills served only briefly in 1868, Dr. Bailey was hired on nine separate occasions between 1871 and 1895 to serve as fort physician. Bailey grew up at Fort Mackinac, where his father, Dr. Joseph Bailey, was post surgeon in the 1850s. After receiving his medical degree from the University of Michigan, Bailey established a private practice on Mackinac Island and made himself available to fort commanders, who depended on his expertise during the frequent vacancies between army-assigned physicians.[61]

Fort Mackinac Abandoned

As soldiers increasingly enjoyed life at Fort Mackinac, army administrators grew ever more skeptical of its military worth. They had the same opinion of Fort Mackinac as tourists—it was a charming curiosity, and little more. In an effort to save money and consolidate troops, the army abandoned dozens of small, less-strategic forts beginning in the late 1880s. By 1892 the army manned only 96 forts, down from a post–Civil War high of 255 forts in 1869.[62] Fort Mackinac dodged the fatal bullet for several years because it provided administrative support for the national park. But at a cost of $40,000 to $50,000 a year, the old fort eventually became a sitting target for sharp-eyed army budget trimmers. The first cut came in November 1892, when Company D, 19th Infantry, was sent to Fort Brady. Two years later Secretary of War Daniel Lamont withdrew most of the remaining troops. Lieutenant Woodbridge Geary and a squad of 11 men stayed behind until the government decided on the final disposition of the fort and national park. Lamont's proposal to sell park lands shocked local citizens, who scurried to preserve their island and found a willing advocate in Senator James McMillan. McMillan led the effort to save the park by transferring it to the State of Michigan. Congress approved the transfer in March 1895. Six months later Lieutenant Geary and his small squad of soldiers marched out of Fort Mackinac for the last time.

Fort Mackinac was a dominant presence on Mackinac Island for over a century. Indeed, the fort and its soldiers had a profound impact on the settlement, growth, evolution, and history of the Mackinac Island community. This includes the layout of the village and military reservation, construction of roads and trails, preservation of natural and cultural resources, location of community cemeteries, and so many of the fascinating stories that form the rich heritage of the island. It has now been more than a century since soldiers departed the fort, but their legacy can be found across the island and is essential to what makes Mackinac so special today.

BRITISH SOLDIERS AT MACKINAC, 1780-1796 AND 1812-1815

Lieutenant Governor Patrick Sinclair

1736–1820

Fort Mackinac was constructed during the American Revolution because of the vision and will of Patrick Sinclair. The 43-year-old native of Lybster, Scotland, was appointed lieutenant governor and superintendent of Michilimackinac in 1775. After several delays, he reached the Straits of Mackinac in 1779 and quickly recognized the vulnerability and defensive limitations of the mainland fort. Fearful of a rebel attack, Sinclair soon began constructing a new fort on Mackinac Island's southern bluff and establishing a civilian community along the shore below the fort. Sinclair spent lavishly constructing the fort, outfitting Indian war parties, and on other Indian Department expenses. In 1782 Sinclair was forced to relinquish his command at Mackinac and travel to Quebec to defend his expenditures.

Silhouette of Sinclair as an older man

Colonel Thomas Aubrey by Nathaniel Hone, 1772

Captain Thomas Aubrey

1740–1814

Thomas Aubrey entered the British army as an ensign in 1762 and served in North America during the Revolution. Aubrey commanded two companies of the 47th Infantry, which successfully defended a supply depot on Diamond Island in Lake George during British Lieutenant General John Burgoyne's 1777 campaign to capture Albany. Ordered to Mackinac Island in the summer of 1781, Captain Aubrey was "much distressed and exceedingly mortified" to learn that he would serve under the command of a junior officer. Nevertheless, Aubrey reported to the island post, and his soldiers helped complete the initial construction of Fort Mackinac prior to leaving one year later.

Captain Gother Mann, 1763

Captain Gother Mann

1747–1830

Gother Mann graduated from the Royal Military Academy at Woolwich (London) in 1763. He served in England and the West Indies prior to being appointed commanding engineer of the Province of Quebec in 1785. Three years later he undertook an extensive examination of British military posts on the Great Lakes. Mann was critical of Fort Mackinac's situation and condition, and concluded that "the greater part of the expense bestowed here has been a waste of money."

William McKay by Levi Stevens, 1816

Captain William McKay

1772–1832

In June 1812 William McKay carried instructions from Major General Isaac Brock to Captain Charles Roberts at Fort St. Joseph regarding the outbreak of hostilities between Great Britain and the United States. By this correspondence, Brock authorized the attack and capture of Fort Mackinac led by Roberts on July 17. In the spring of 1814 McKay was appointed to command the Michigan Fencibles, a provincial corps raised at Mackinac. In this capacity, McKay led a successful expedition against the American post at Prairie du Chien, Wisconsin, a few months later.

Library and Archives Canada, Acc. No. 1989-484-3

Andrew Bulger driving his family on the frozen Red River in a horse cariole with Fort Garry in the background (winter of 1822–1823), by Peter Rindisbacher

Lieutenant Andrew Bulger

1789–1858

Lieutenant Andrew Bulger served in the Royal Newfoundland Regiment and arrived at Mackinac in 1814 with Lieutenant Colonel Robert McDouall. Bulger saw action in the American attack against Mackinac on August 4, 1814, and was slightly wounded during the daring capture of the American schooners *Tigress* and *Scorpion* in early September. One month later, Bulger was appointed commandant of Fort McKay, at Prairie du Chien. In 1821 Bulger was selected to serve as secretary of the Red River Settlement, Manitoba, a post he left two years later.

Dumfries and Galloway Museums Service, Stranraer Museum

General Robert McDouall, ca. 1812

Lieutenant Colonel Robert McDouall

1774–1848

McDouall was born in Stranraer, Scotland, in 1774 and purchased an ensigncy in the British army 23 years later. He served with the 8th Regiment of Foot and saw service in Egypt and Martinique before coming to Canada in 1810. During the War of 1812 McDouall was promoted and assigned to the Glengarry Light Infantry Fencibles, a Scottish unit raised in Canada. McDouall was appointed brevet lieutenant colonel in July 1813 and given command of Fort Mackinac the following spring. McDouall successfully defended Fort Mackinac during the American assault in the summer of 1814, only to surrender the fort a year later as a result of the terms of the Treaty of Ghent. In February 1817, McDouall was appointed a Companion of the Order of the Bath for his efforts at Mackinac.

U.S. SOLDIERS AT MACKINAC, 1796-1812

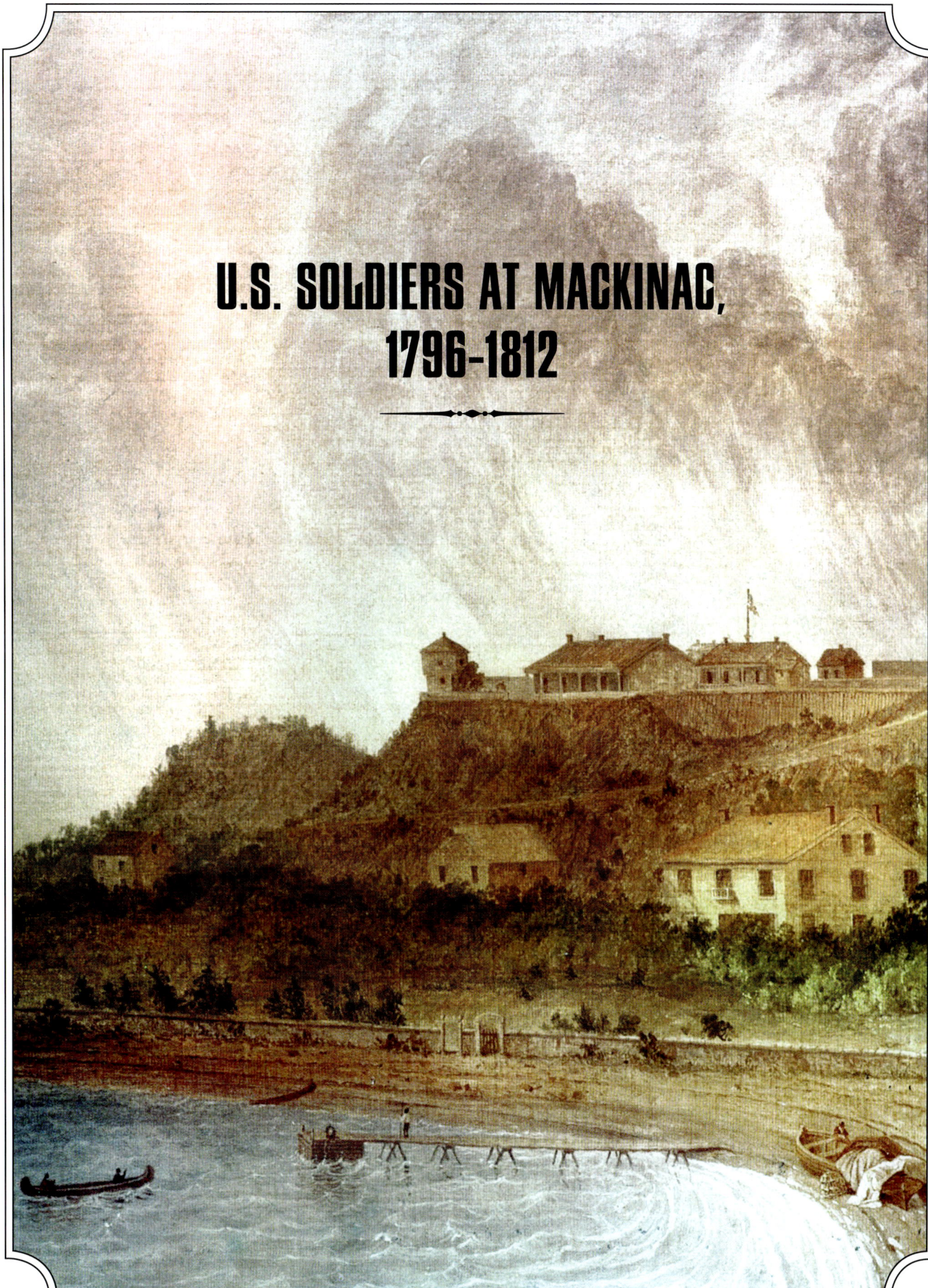

Courtesy of Fraunces Tavern® Museum, New York City

General Henry Burbeck, John Trumbull (attributed)

Major Henry Burbeck

1754–1848

Henry Burbeck began his career as an artillery officer during the American Revolution and continued to serve in the army through the War of 1812. Following service in the Indian Wars of the 1790s, Burbeck led the first American soldiers into Fort Mackinac in September 1796. A week after his arrival, Burbeck wrote, "I find this place abounds with good health, rocks and fish (Marblehead), that's the most I can say of it." During his three-year command, Burbeck and his troops substantially rebuilt the post, replacing the old British bastions with stone and heavy timber blockhouses and incorporating the north ravelin into the defensive perimeter of the fort. This general configuration remained throughout the fort's occupation.

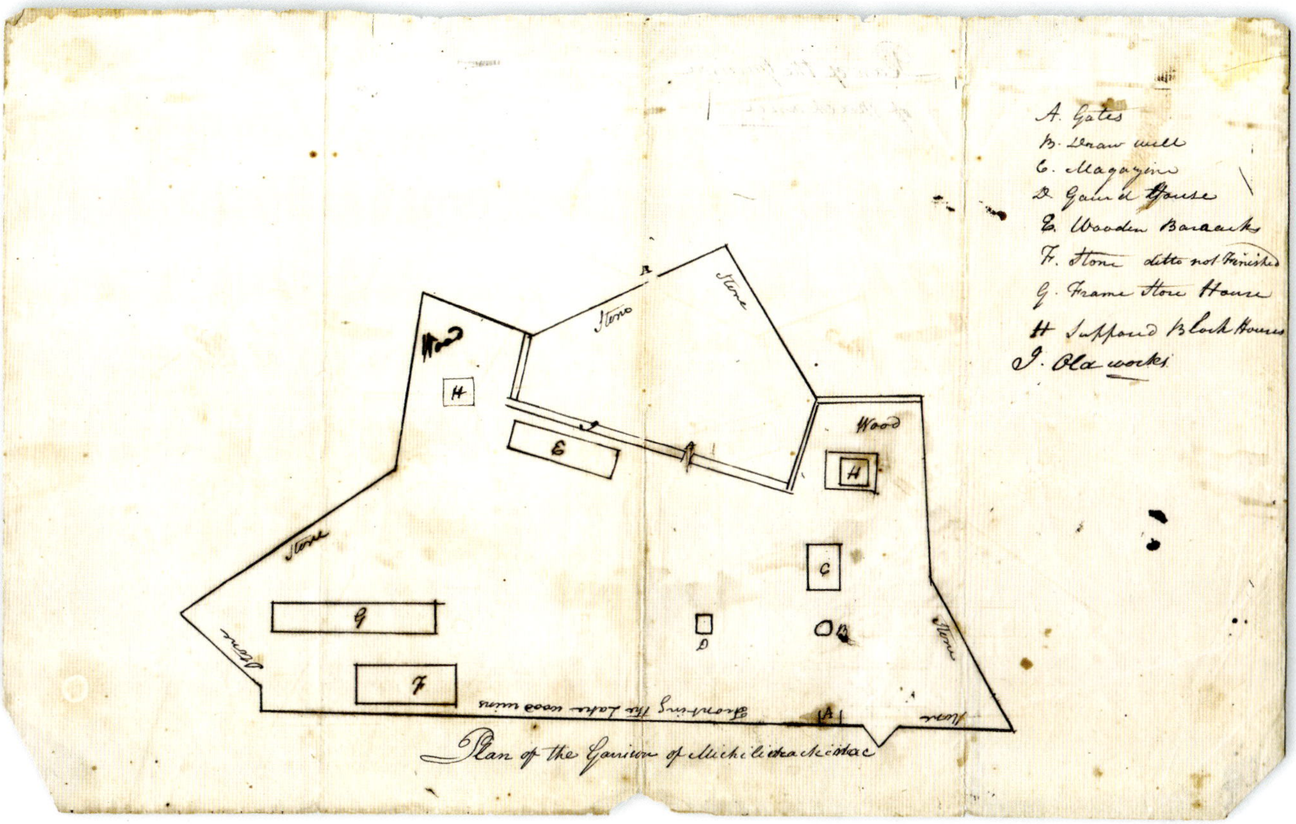

Plan of Fort Mackinac, 1797

General James Wilkinson traveled to Mackinac Island in the summer of 1797 to inspect the fort and decide how it should be reconfigured. Wilkinson declined the suggestion that the fort should be reduced in size. Instead, he ordered substantial repairs and the construction of two blockhouses, marked "H" on the plan that he presented to Major Burbeck. These improvements, argued Wilkinson, would render Fort Mackinac "impregnable to the attacks of small armys."

Portrait of Richard Whiley, unknown artist, ca. 1810, from a color print produced in 1922

Mackinac State Historic Parks, Acc. No. 2015.123.1

Courtesy of Crum & Forster, photo courtesy of the William L. Clements Library. The portrait was used by artist Julio Kilenyi to create the medallion that was struck by Whitehead & Hoag in 1922 on the 100th anniversary of the North River Insurance Company (New Jersey).

Lieutenant Richard Whiley

ca. 1770–1847

Richard Whiley began his military service as an enlisted man in the Dragoons during the Indian Wars of the 1790s. He was appointed lieutenant in the Artillerists and Engineers in December 1796 and arrived at Fort Mackinac the following year. In 1799, the army removed most of the soldiers from Fort Mackinac, leaving Whiley and a small detachment of 35 artillerists and infantrymen to garrison the post. That year, Lieutenant George Landmann, a British officer stationed at nearby Fort St. Joseph, described Whiley as "a young, fair, beardless personage, on good terms with himself and placed great reliance for his military dignity on the length of his boots and the thickness of his queue." Whiley remained at Mackinac until 1802 and resigned his commission in 1811. In 1822 he founded the North River Insurance Company.

Courtesy of Danvers Archival Center, Danvers, MA

General Moses Porter, ca. 1814–1821

Captain Moses Porter

1756–1822

Born in Boston in 1756, Moses Porter served as an artillery officer during the American Revolution. Porter led the U.S. soldiers that peacefully occupied Detroit on July 11, 1796, when the post was transferred from British control as a result of the Jay Treaty. The following summer Porter joined the rest of his company of artillerists and engineers at Fort Mackinac, where he supervised the rebuilding of the fort over the next two years. Porter later served as a regimental commander of light artillery during the War of 1812 and was promoted brevet brigadier general in 1813 "for distinguished service" during the war. Porter died while still in the service in 1822.

Oil-on-tinned-iron portrait of Thomas Hunt, ca. 1808

Lieutenant Colonel Thomas Hunt

1754–1808

Fort Mackinac became a two-company post when President Thomas Jefferson reorganized the army in 1802 and concentrated troops on the frontier and at seacoast batteries and federal arsenals. As a result, Fort Mackinac, under the command of Lieutenant Colonel Thomas Hunt, became the nation's six largest military installation, with over 120 soldiers in 1803. Hunt's son, Samuel Wellington Hunt, returned to Fort Mackinac as an infantry officer in 1823. Hunt's daughter, Mary Le Barron Hunt, born at Mackinac in 1802 and delivered by post surgeon Dr. Francis Le Barron, returned to Fort Mackinac in 1820 as the wife of Lieutenant Joseph Gleason.

Courtesy of the Plymouth Antiquarian Society

Portrait miniature of Dr. Francis Le Barron, attributed to Thomas Sully

Dr. Francis Le Barron

1781–1829

Dr. Francis Le Barron began his military medical career as a surgeon's mate in the U.S. Navy in 1800. Two years later he transferred to the army and became the first in a long line of U.S. medical officers to serve Fort Mackinac. During his tenure at Mackinac, Dr. Le Barron constructed a distillery on property along the shore west of the village. Island citizens took refuge in this building during the British attack at the outbreak of the War of 1812. Le Barron served as the U.S. Army's apothecary general during the War of 1812 and remained in the office until it was eliminated in the army reduction act of 1821.

Portrait of Jacob Kingsbury, 1813, by Samuel Lovett Waldo (1783–1861)

Lieutenant Colonel Jacob Kingsbury

1756–1837

Jacob Kingsbury served as an enlisted man and officer with the Connecticut Continental Infantry during the American Revolution. Following the war, Kingsbury was appointed to the 1st U.S. Infantry and arrived at Fort Mackinac as a lieutenant colonel. He commanded the post in 1804–1805. Kingsbury lived with his wife Sally Ellis, son James Wilkinson, and infant daughter Julia in the officers' stone quarters. Soon after arriving, Kingsbury described the island post as "one of the pleasantest situations I know of in the United States; but one thing against it, severe cold." Kingsbury's nephew, Lieutenant Julius Jesse Bronson Kingsbury, served at Fort Mackinac in 1833–1836.

Miniature portrait of
Lieutenant Presley O'Bannon

Lieutenant Presley Neville O'Bannon, Tripolitan War, 1805, a sketch by Neville Cain (1855–1935)

Lieutenant Presley Neville O'Bannon

1776–1850

Lieutenant Presley O'Bannon served in the U.S. Marines and distinguished himself in the Tripoli Campaign during the First Barbary War (1801–1805). O'Bannon became the first man to raise a U.S. flag over foreign soil in time of war at the Battle of Derna on April 27, 1805. O'Bannon resigned from the Marines in 1807, received a commission in the U.S. Army, and commanded Fort Mackinac during the winter of 1807–1808.

Mackinac State Historic Parks, Acc. No. 1985.8.1, gift of Kay Kendall-Krapill

Artillery officer's sword belonging to Lieutenant Porter Hanks, L. Wells and Company, New York

Lieutenant Porter Hanks

ca. 1785–1812

Massachusetts-born Porter Hanks was appointed to the U.S. Army, Corps of Artillery, on January 17, 1805. Hanks arrived at Fort Mackinac in 1808 with a company of artillerists under the command of Captain Lewis Howard. Hanks assumed command of the island post after Howard died in February 1811. Seventeen months later, Hanks surrendered Fort Mackinac to British troops at the outbreak of the War of 1812. Hanks was sent to Detroit to face a court of inquiry regarding his decision to surrender. It was here that Hanks was killed during the British bombardment of Detroit on August 16, 1812.

Courtesy Vermont Historical Society

Dr. Sylvester Day, 1840s

Dr. Sylvester Day

1778–1851

Dr. Sylvester Day received a warrant as a surgeon's mate in 1807 and was posted to Fort Mackinac three years later. Dr. Day was living in the village below the fort when invading British troops landed on the north end of the island. After witnessing civilians fleeing to the safety of Le Barron's distillery, Day ran to the fort to warn the American commander, Lieutenant Porter Hanks, of the impending attack. Following the war, Day remained in the army and served at a variety of posts in Michigan, Pennsylvania, New York, and Maine. He died on duty at Allegheny Arsenal in Pittsburgh in 1851.

U.S. SOLDIERS AT MACKINAC, 1815-1861

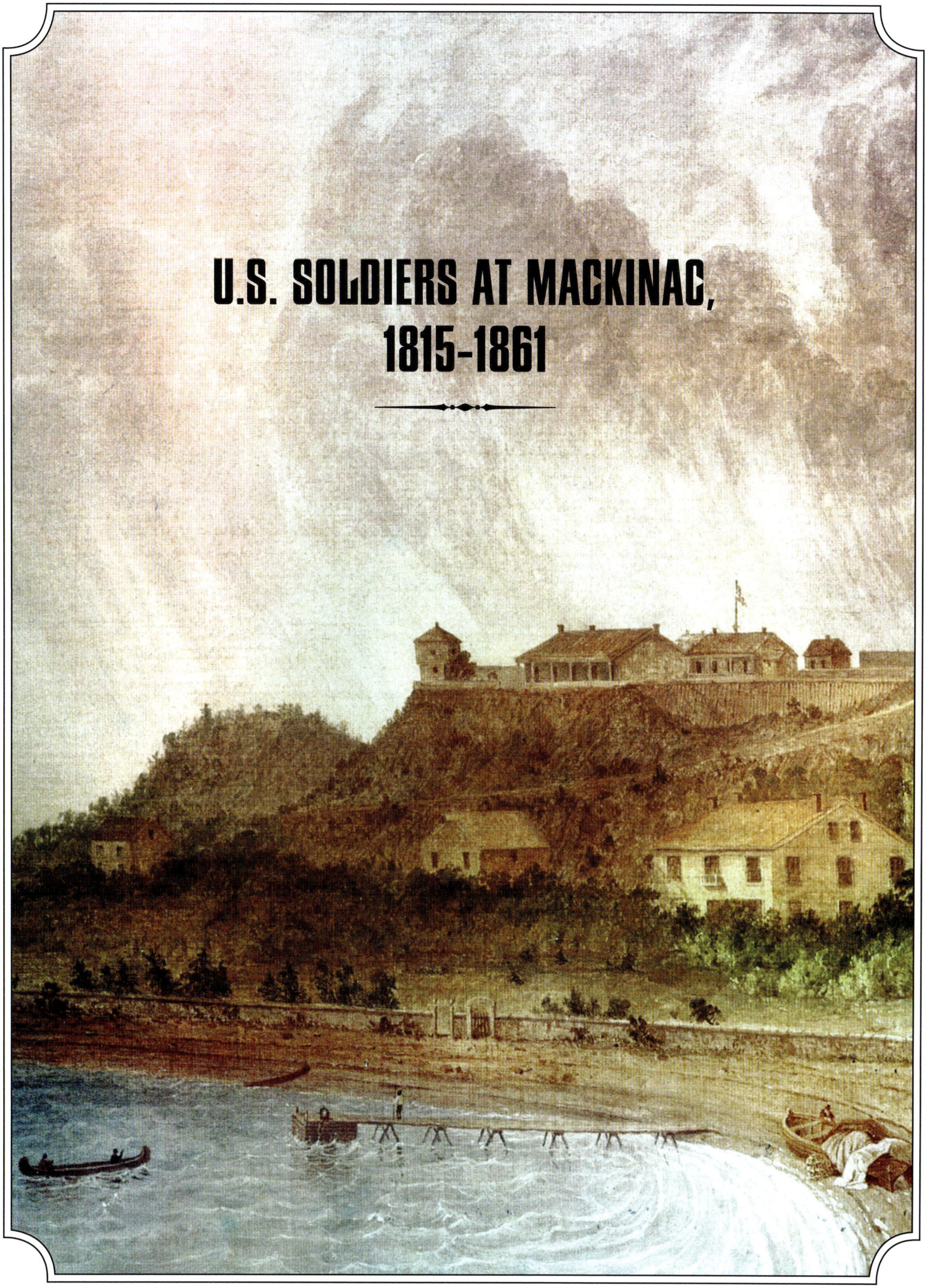

Missouri History Museum, St. Louis

Mid-nineteenth-century engraving of John O'Fallon as a wealthy St. Louis businessman

Captain John O'Fallon

1791–1865

Kentucky-born John O'Fallon received an appointment as an ensign at the outbreak of the War of 1812 and served with both infantry and rifle companies during the conflict. O'Fallon remained in the army after the war and commanded a company of riflemen at Mackinac beginning in 1815. He left the service in 1817 and moved to St. Louis, where he became assistant Indian agent to his uncle William Clark, of Lewis and Clark expedition fame. O'Fallon eventually amassed great wealth selling supplies to the army and launching the Pacific Railroad in 1849.

Mackinac State Historic Parks

Benjamin K. Pierce, ca. 1825

Captain Benjamin K. Pierce

1790–1850

Captain Benjamin Kendrick Pierce arrived at Fort Mackinac shortly after the end of the War of 1812 and remained at the island post until 1821. Pierce married Josette, daughter of prominent Mackinac Island fur trader Magdelaine LaFramboise, in 1816. Josette died in childbirth four years later, leaving Pierce with two young children. Pierce was joined at Fort Mackinac by his half-sister, Elizabeth, when she arrived with her husband, Major John McNeil in 1816, and his brother, Lieutenant John Pierce, who briefly served at Mackinac in 1817. Their younger brother, Franklin, was elected 14th president of the United States in 1853. Benjamin saw service in the Second Seminole War (1835–1842), and Fort Pierce, Florida, was named in his honor.

Columbia Photo Collection, The State Historical Society of Missouri

Missouri governor John Miller (1826–1832)

Colonel John Miller

1781–1846

A native of Berkeley County, Virginia (now West Virginia), John Miller was commissioned from civilian life into the U.S. 17th Regiment of Infantry as a lieutenant at the outbreak of the War of 1812. Miller led troops into battle during the American defense of Fort Meigs (Ohio) in 1813. During the engagement Miller captured a British gun battery outside the fort, only to be repulsed and forced back into the fort by British troops under Captain Richard Bullock. A few months later, Bullock and his troops were sent to Mackinac, where he commanded the island fort until May 1814. Miller commanded Fort Mackinac in 1816 following the American reoccupation of the post after the war. He resigned his commission in 1818 and began a political career in Missouri that culminated in his election as governor from 1826 to 1832. Miller died in 1846 and was buried in the private vault of his wealthy friend John O'Fallon, with whom he served at Fort Mackinac 30 years earlier.

Courtesy of the West Point Museum Collection, U.S. Military Academy

Brevet Brigadier General Charles Gratiot, 1830, by Thomas Sully

Major Charles Gratiot

1788–1855

Charles Gratiot attended the U.S. Military Academy at West Point in 1804–1806 and was soon after commissioned second lieutenant in the Corps of Engineers. During the War of 1812, Gratiot participated in the effort to capture Fort Mackinac in 1814 and served as adjutant to expedition leader Lieutenant Colonel George Croghan. Although never assigned to Fort Mackinac, Gratiot spent considerable time at the island post in 1816–1817 surveying and drawing Fort Mackinac and Fort Holmes.

MacLean Collection

Michilimackinac 1817, by Major Francis S. Belton

Major Francis Smith Belton, an assistant inspector general stationed in Detroit, visited Mackinac Island during an inspection tour of Great Lakes forts in the summer of 1817. This pencil-and-watercolor wash clearly depicts island topography and the relationship between the village, Fort Mackinac, and Fort Holmes. This is the only known image showing both forts under occupation by U.S. soldiers. A portion of the north stockade wall that originally protected the village was still standing when Belton did this drawing.

Colonel John Garland, 8th U.S. Infantry, ca. 1860

Lieutenant John Garland

1793–1861

Virginia native John Garland was a career military officer whose service extended from the War of 1812 through the beginning of the Civil War. Garland was stationed with the 3rd Regiment of Infantry at Fort Mackinac for a brief period beginning in 1816. Garland saw extensive combat during the Mexican-American War and was severely wounded while leading his brigade into Mexico City. In 1848, Lieutenant James Longstreet married Garland's daughter and named his firstborn son John Garland Longstreet in honor of his father-in-law. Longstreet resigned his commission and joined the Confederate army at the outbreak of the Civil War, while Garland remained loyal to the Union.

General John McNeil, ca. 1825–1835, by Henry Willard (1800–1857)

Colonel John McNeil Jr.

1784–1850

A native of New Hampshire, John McNeil was commissioned as a captain in the 11th Infantry just before the outbreak of the War of 1812. McNeil distinguished himself during the war when he led a bayonet charge that secured the American victory in the Battle of Chippawa, and during the Battle of Bridgewater, where he was severely wounded. Colonel John McNeil took command of Fort Mackinac in October 1816. One month later, the garrison swelled to 355 men, the largest contingent to ever serve at Fort Mackinac. Less than a year later McNeil transferred command of the post to his brother-in-law Captain Benjamin Pierce when he was reassigned to Fort Gratiot, at Port Huron, Michigan.

Major William Whistler, ca. 1830, by Grove Shelden Gilbert

Mackinac State Historic Parks, Acc. No. 2007.4.1

Silver pectoral owned by William Whistler. The image commemorates the surrender of Winnebago chief Red Bird to Whistler, then commander at Green Bay, during the "Winnebago War" of 1827.

Mackinac State Historic Parks, Acc. No. 2007.4.3

Captain William Whistler

1783–1863

William Whistler was commissioned as an officer in the army in 1801. During his 60-year career, Whistler served at Mackinac three times, in 1816, 1823, and 1833, the last two as commandant. The portrait by Gilbert was likely done while Whistler was stationed at Fort Niagara (1828–1832) and traveled with him to Mackinac. The portrait hung in his home in the officers' stone quarters. Whistler was the uncle of James Abbott McNeill Whistler, the famous artist best known for his portrait *Whistler's Mother*.

William Lawrence, portrait by B. Gettier, 1969, based on an original from the 1830s

Colonel William Lawrence

1770–1847

William Lawrence joined the U.S. Army in 1801 and served during the War of 1812 as a captain in the 2nd Regiment of Infantry. Lawrence commanded and successfully defended Fort Boyer, a strategic fortification near the mouth of Mobile Bay (Alabama), during the British assault in September 1814. Lawrence remained in the army after the war and commanded Fort Mackinac in 1819–1821.

Mackinac State Historic Parks

Dr. William Beaumont, ca. 1825

Dr. William Beaumont

1785–1853

Dr. William Beaumont served as post surgeon at Fort Mackinac from 1820 to 1825. Beaumont treated Alexis St. Martin, a 19-year old French-Canadian voyageur, when he was accidently shot in 1822. Beaumont nursed the young man back to health, but a permanent hole remained in St. Martin's abdomen. Beaumont took advantage of this unusual opportunity to perform experiments on St. Martin's stomach. Through these studies, begun in his residence in the officers' stone quarters, Beaumont furthered the scientific understanding of human digestion. Dr. Beaumont retired from the army in 1839 and lived the rest of his life in St. Louis, Missouri where he had a successful medical practice until his death in 1853.

Special Collections Research Center, University of Chicago Library

William and Deborah Beaumont with children (*left to right*) Lucretia, Sarah, and Israel, 1832

Roger Hunt Collection, U.S. Army Heritage and Education Center, Carlisle, PA

Lieutenant Colonel George H. Crosman, departmental quartermaster, ca. 1860

Lieutenant George Hampden Crosman

1799–1882

George Crosman graduated from West Point in 1823 and served with the 6th Regiment of Infantry at Fort Mackinac that summer. Crosman fought in the Black Hawk and Mexican-American wars and served in the Quartermaster Department during the Civil War. Following the war, Crosman compiled the "Manual for the Quartermaster Department," published in March 1866, and retired as brevet brigadier general later that year.

General Richard Satterlee, ca. 1865

Dr. Richard S. Satterlee

1796–1880

Richard S. Satterlee replaced William Beaumont as Fort Mackinac's post surgeon in 1825. Dr. Satterlee remained at the island fort until 1831, except for a brief furlough in 1827. A native of New York state, Satterlee practiced medicine in Detroit before joining the army in 1822. While at Fort Mackinac, Satterlee wrote the surgeon general complaining about the "ravages of whiskey" made available through army rations and for sale in the post sutler's store. Complaining that "very many of the diseases in the army arise from the abuse of ardent spirits," Satterlee suggested that the "whiskey ration be stopped and an equivalent given in money." This, combined with removing "spirituous liquors" from the sutler's store, would result in "more sober, healthy, and much more effective men." Satterlee subsequently served as a medical officer in the Second Seminole and Mexican-American wars and as a medical purveyor during the Civil War. He was promoted brevet brigadier general in 1864 for his service to the Union army.

Massachusetts Mollus Photograph Collection, U.S. Army Heritage and Education Center, Carlisle, PA

Carlos A. Waite, ca. 1864

Lieutenant Carlos A. Waite

1797–1866

Second Lieutenant Carlos Adolphus Waite was stationed briefly at Fort Mackinac in 1825–1826. After serving in the Quartermaster's Department from 1838 to 1845, Waite was appointed major in the 8th Infantry and took active field service during the Mexican-American War. Waite led troops into battle at Contreras, Churubusco, and Molino del Rey, where he was severely wounded. Waite retired in 1864 and was promoted brevet brigadier general in 1865 for "long and faithful service in the Army of the United States."

Mackinac State Historic Parks, photograph courtesy of Linda Zimmermann

Major Alexander Thompson, ca. 1835

Major Alexander Ramsay Thompson
1793–1837

Major Alexander Thompson attended the U.S. Military Academy at West Point from 1810 to 1812 and was commissioned first lieutenant in the 6th Regiment of Infantry just before the War of 1812. Following the war, Thompson served at various posts and on recruiting duty before being assigned to Mackinac. Thompson commanded Fort Mackinac in 1826–1828 and oversaw a massive construction project that significantly improved the post. As Thompson was coming to the end of his work, army inspector Colonel George Croghan predicted that Fort Mackinac would soon "be esteemed the most desirable of our infantry posts." After serving at Fort Gratiot for four years, Thompson returned to command the island fort in 1832–1833. Thompson was killed in action at Okeechobee, Florida, in 1837 during the Second Seminole War.

Scan No. PH.PROP.3564 History Colorado

Dr. Edwin James, from a miniature on ivory in possession of the family, reproduced in *Annals of Iowa*, October 1907

Dr. Edwin James

1797–1861

Dr. Edwin James joined the U.S. Army as an assistant surgeon in 1823 and served at Fort Mackinac during Dr. Satterlee's furlough in 1827. While at Mackinac, James assisted John Tanner in writing his book, *A Narrative of the Captivity and Adventures of John Tanner*, which was published 1830. Prior to his service in the army, James served as botanist on Major Stephen Long's 1819–1820 expedition to the Rocky Mountains, where he amassed an extensive collection of mountain plants. Fellow botanist Charles C. Parry described James as "tall, erect, with a benevolent expression of countenance, and a piercing black eye."

U.S. Army Heritage and Education Center

Major General Edwin Sumner, ca. 1862

Lieutenant Edwin Vose Sumner

1797–1863

Edwin Vose Sumner had a short and unhappy stay at Fort Mackinac. The 30-year-old lieutenant was transferred to Company A, 2nd Infantry, at Fort Mackinac in the fall of 1827 to fill the vacancy created by the death of Lieutenant David Brooks. On February 20, 1828, Sumner was arrested for his conduct toward post surgeon Dr. Richard Satterlee. Sumner was eventually sent to Fort Howard, Green Bay, where he faced a general court-martial. Found guilty of the charge in the summer of 1828, Sumner was suspended from the army for six months. Upon reinstatement, Sumner was transferred to 1st Regiment of Dragoons and served with distinction in the Mexican-American War. It was during the Battle of Cerro Gordo in April 1847 that Sumner gained the nickname "Bull Head" after a musket ball bounced off his head. Sumner was promoted to major general of volunteers during the Civil War.

Major General Samuel Heintzelman, ca. 1863

Massachusetts Mollus Photograph Collection, U.S. Army Heritage and Education Center, Carlisle, PA

Lieutenant Samuel Peter Heintzelman

1805–1880

An 1826 graduate of West Point, Lieutenant Samuel Heintzelman served at Fort Mackinac in 1827–1828. Heintzelman kept a detailed journal throughout his life, and the entries during his time at Mackinac provide a rare and illuminating view into life at the island fort in the late 1820s. Heintzelman saw extensive combat duty during his career, including service in the Seminole War, the Mexican-American War, and the Yuma War. Heintzelman was a prominent figure in the early months of the Civil War and served as commander of the Third Corps in the Union Army of the Potomac during the Peninsula Campaign.

Josiah H. Vose, ca. 1832–1845

Major Josiah Howe Vose

1784–1845

Josiah Vose joined the U.S. Army as a captain in the 21st Regiment of Infantry on April 9, 1812. During the War of 1812, Vose led troops during the invasion of Canada at the battles of Chippawa and Lundy's Lane. Vose was retained in the postwar army and assigned various duties in the following years, including recruiting service, garrison duty, and construction of military roads in the Indiana Territory. Major Vose briefly served as post commandant at Fort Mackinac from November 1828 through April 1829, just a few months after his nephew, Lieutenant Edwin Vose Sumner, was suspended by general court-martial.

Captain Ephraim Kirby Smith, ca. 1838–1847

Lieutenant Ephraim Kirby Smith

1807–1847

Ephraim Kirby Smith graduated (last in his class) from the U.S. Military Academy at West Point in 1826. Fort Mackinac was his second assignment, and it was here that he was involved in the "Christmas Day Mutiny" of 1829. Court-martialed for inflicting physical punishment on several soldiers, Smith was convicted and dismissed from the army in 1830. Eighteen months later, President Andrew Jackson restored Smith's commission in the army. Smith died on September 11, 1847, as a result of wounds received at the Battle of Molino del Rey during the Mexican-American War. One year earlier, noted landscape architect Frederick Law Olmsted described Smith as a, "tall, straight, well-made man, with an honest, frank, sun-burnt face, short curly hair, and handsome whiskers."

Chicago History Museum, ICHi88685

Louis T. Jamison, artist unknown, ca, 1835

Lieutenant Louis Thornton Jamison

1805–1858

Virginia-born Louis Thornton Jamison entered the army as a second lieutenant in 1824. A West Point graduate, Jamison served less than a year before he resigned his commission. A few months later, Jamison returned to the army and was stationed at several forts before briefly serving at Mackinac in the fall of 1829. Jamison was dismissed from the army for financial irregularities in 1838 but returned to Fort Mackinac as a civilian post sutler in 1840 and continued in the position until 1846. Jamison carried a wide assortment of goods in his fort store, including food and spirits, clothing and grooming accessories, and dishes and tools.

Roger Hunt Collection, U.S. Army Heritage and Education Center, Carlisle, PA

Lieutenant Colonel Caleb C. Sibley, 9th Regiment U.S. Infantry. It is presumed that the woman on the left is his wife, Nancy Davenport Sibley, ca. 1861–1864.

Lieutenant Caleb Chase Sibley

1806–1875

Caleb Chase Sibley graduated from West Point in 1829, and his first duty assignment was at Fort Mackinac. While at Mackinac, Sibley married Nancy Davenport in a ceremony led by Rev. William Ferry at the newly constructed Mission Church on May 18, 1831. Nancy was the daughter of Ambrose Davenport, who came to the island in 1796 as a sergeant with the first American troops to occupy Fort Mackinac. Following his assignment at Fort Mackinac, Sibley served in various posts and campaigns across the country. He was in command of Fort McIntosh, Texas, at the outbreak of the Civil War and was forced to surrender the post to an overwhelming Confederate force. Sibley remained in the regular army through the war and was promoted brevet brigadier general in 1865.

Courtesy of the Neville Public Museum of Brown County

Captain Moses Emery Merrill, ca. 1845

Captain Moses Merrill

1804–1847

After graduating from West Point in 1826, Moses Merrill spent 19 years serving at various frontier posts, including Fort Mackinac (1829, 1830–1831, 1843–1845). While at Mackinac in 1830, Merrill found military duty dull and routine, but enjoyed the social opportunities available to a young, single officer. On February 2 he wrote, "I have spent a considerable part of my time in the society of about half a dozen Ladies (Widows and young Ladies) quite select I assure you, sometimes in a pleasant *tete a tete*, and other times, as often as the weather will permit, taking a sleigh ride across the Island and back, and by the way of a call, stop at our neighbors, or extending our ride a few miles on the straits." Merrill married Louisa Slaughter in Green Bay in 1836, and they lived together in the east apartment of the hill quarters during his final stay at Fort Mackinac. Merrill was killed in action in September 1847 at the Battle of Molino del Rey during the Mexican-American War.

U.S. Military Academy Cadet Edgar M. Lacey, drawing by Cadet F. Harrison Jr., May 4, 1826

Lieutenant Edgar M. Lacey

1806–1839

Edgar Martin Lacey graduated from West Point in 1827 and joined the 5th Regiment of Infantry the same year. While stationed at Fort Howard, Green Bay, Wisconsin, Lieutenant Lacey was ordered to serve on the general court convened at Fort Mackinac for the trial of the eight enlisted men charged for their participation in the "Christmas Day Mutiny" of 1829. Bored with the proceedings of the case, Lacey wrote his sister on May 31, 1830, complaining, "I find myself at this dull, sanctified place with nothing to do." Lacey died while stationed at Fort Crawford, Wisconsin, in 1839 at age 33.

Theodore Brooke

Lieutenant Colonel George Mercer Brooke, artist unknown, ca. 1825

Colonel and Brevet Brigadier General George Mercer Brooke

1785–1851

George M. Brooke was born in Virginia and appointed first lieutenant in the U.S. Army in 1808. Brooke served on the New York frontier during the War of 1812. He remained in the army following the war and was appointed colonel and regimental commander of the 5th Regiment of Infantry in 1831. Brooke commanded Fort Mackinac from May through October 1832, a period during which the fur trade was still the dominant industry of the upper Great Lakes. Brooke was the highest-ranking officer to serve at Fort Mackinac during its final 63 years of occupation. Colonel Brooke was engaged in staff duties in Texas during the Mexican-American War and died in San Antonio in 1851.

Captain George W. Patten, with daughter Ada and son George W. Jr., in 1846

Lieutenant George W. Patten

1808–1882

In 1830 George Waynefleet Patten received a master of arts degree from Brown University (Rhode Island) and graduated from West Point. He was assigned as a second lieutenant with the 2nd Regiment of Infantry and posted to Fort Mackinac in 1832–1833. Patten served in the Mexican-American War, where he was severely wounded, losing his left hand, during the Battle of Cerro Gordo in 1847. Patten performed garrison and staff duties during the Civil War and retired from active duty in 1864.

Massachusetts Mollus Photograph Collection, U.S. Army Heritage and Education Center, Carlisle, PA

Joseph Rowe Smith, ca. 1860

Lieutenant Joseph Rowe Smith

1802–1868

First Lieutenant Joseph R. Smith served at Fort Mackinac with Company B, 2nd Infantry, in 1832–1833. A native of Sandy Hill, New York and a graduate of West Point, Smith was severely wounded at the Battle of Churubusco during the Mexican-American War. These wounds, compounded by an illness contracted in Florida during the Second Seminole War, forced Smith to take a disability retirement in 1861. During the Civil War, Smith served in a noncombat role as a mustering officer for the State of Michigan. His son, Dr. Joseph Rowe Smith Jr., joined the army in 1854 and was later appointed chief assistant to the surgeon general of the U.S. Army, Dr. William A. Hammond (who was post surgeon at Fort Mackinac, 1859–1860) during the Civil War.

www.santafetrailresearch.com/trail-photo-02/walnut-creek-portraits.html

Colonel Jesse H. Leavenworth

Lieutenant Jesse H. Leavenworth

1807–1885

The son of General Henry Leavenworth (after whom Leavenworth, Kansas, and Leavenworth Penitentiary are named), Jesse graduated from West Point in 1830 and served only six years in the regular army. His last posting was at Fort Mackinac (1833–1836), after which he worked as a civil engineer from 1836 to 1858. Leavenworth was commissioned colonel in the Colorado volunteers during the Civil War, after which he served as U.S. Indian agent for the southern Cheyenne, Kiowa, and Comanche Indian tribes.

Massachusetts Mollus Photograph Collection, U.S. Army Heritage and Education Center, Carlisle, PA

Lieutenant Colonel James V. Bomford, 16th Regiment, U.S. Infantry, in civilian dress

Lieutenant James Vote Bomford

1811–1892

James Vote Bomford graduated from West Point in 1832 and was assigned to Fort Mackinac with the 2nd Infantry two years later. Bomford saw extensive combat action throughout his 42-year military career, including service in the Black Hawk and Seminole wars. He participated in all of the major battles of the Mexican-American War and planted the first American flag at the citadel in Mexico City in 1847. Bomford was taken prisoner by Confederate troops while on command at Fort Davis, Texas, at the outbreak of the Civil War. Once exchanged, he saw extensive action with the U.S. 16th Infantry and was wounded twice during the Battle of Perryville, Kentucky. Bomford retired as a brigadier general in 1872.

William Chapman, ca. 1836, oil painting by Alfred Jacob Miller (1810–1874)

Abby Ann Wheelock Chapman, ca. 1836, oil portrait by Alfred Jacob Miller (1810–1874)

Captain William Chapman (*left*) with another soldier (thought to be Captain Moses Merrill), April 1847, Mexico

Lieutenant William Chapman

1810–1887

William Chapman graduated from West Point in 1831 and briefly served with Company G, 5th Infantry, at Fort Mackinac the following year. Chapman met and married Abby Ann Wheelock in 1836 while stationed at Fort Howard (Green Bay). Chapman returned to the island post in 1841 and lived there with Abby for four years before being assigned to Texas and, in 1846, service in the Mexican-American War. In a letter to his mother, dated May 12, 1843, Chapman expressed the joyful enthusiasm that accompanied the end of a long winter at Mackinac: "The opening of navigation after a long and tedious winter has revived the spirits of our little community and our streets present quite a business appearance. We have had but one steamboat as yet, but are hourly expecting another." Chapman served with distinction in the Civil War through the Second Battle of Bull Run and retired from active service in August 1863.

William Chapman, during the Civil War, ca. 1862

Brigadier General Marsena Patrick, ca. 1863

Massachusetts Mollus Photograph Collection, U.S. Army Heritage and Education Center, Carlisle, PA

Lieutenant Marsena R. Patrick

1811–1888

Lieutenant Marsena Patrick's first duty assignment after graduating from West Point in 1835 was Fort Mackinac. While stationed at Mackinac, Patrick married Mary McGulpin in a ceremony performed by Justice of the Peace Jonathan King on October 10, 1836. Patrick participated in the field during the Second Seminole War in Florida and during the Mexican-American War. Patrick resigned his commission in 1850 and operated a farm near Sackett's Harbor, New York, until the outbreak of the Civil War, when he was appointed brigadier general of the New York State Volunteers. From 1862 to 1865 Patrick served as provost marshal general in the Army of the Potomac, responsible for a wide variety of tasks, mostly related to troop discipline. He left the service after the war and subsequently served as president of the New York State Agricultural College and, in 1871, director of the Soldier's Home in Dayton, Ohio.

Photograph courtesy of the Milwaukee County Historical Society

Dr. Erastus B. Wolcott

Dr. Erastus Bradley Wolcott

1804–1880

New York native Erastus B. Wolcott was commissioned first lieutenant and assistant surgeon on January 1, 1836, and immediately traveled to Fort Mackinac, where he arrived on February 10. Just two months later, after a whirlwind courtship, Wolcott married Elizabeth Jane Dousman, the 18-year-old daughter of Michael Dousman, a prominent and successful Mackinac Island merchant. Wolcott resigned his commission in 1839 and moved to Milwaukee, where he helped found both the Wisconsin state and Milwaukee medical societies. Dr. Wolcott was the Wisconsin state surgeon general during the Civil War and is credited with having performed the first surgical kidney removal in 1861.

Massachusetts Mollus Photograph Collection, U.S. Army Heritage and Education Center, Carlisle, PA

Brevet Brigadier General Harvey Brown, ca. 1862

Captain Harvey Brown

1795–1874

Soldiers from the 4th Regiment of Artillery, led by Captain Harvey Brown, permanently reoccupied Fort Mackinac in May 1840, three years after it was abandoned during the Second Seminole War. Brown, with a small contingent of 41 artillerists, undertook the task of reopening and fortifying the mothballed fort. Four months later Methodist missionary Rev. John H. Pitezel, impressed with Brown's efforts at maintaining Fort Mackinac, wrote, "We thought it difficult to imagine how anything could be kept in a more neat and orderly manner." After Mackinac, Brown served in the Mexican-American War and Civil War and retired from active duty in 1863 after a 45-year career.

Massachusetts Mollus Photograph Collection, U.S. Army Heritage and Education Center, Carlisle, PA

John Wolcott Phelps, ca. 1862

First Lieutenant John Wolcott Phelps

1813–1885

Lieutenant John W. Phelps arrived in May 1840 with the first contingent of soldiers to occupy Fort Mackinac following the Second Seminole War. One week after his arrival, Phelps reported the successful completion of a number of tasks designed to revive the fort after three years of neglect. Work included repairing collapsed walls, plowing and planting the fort garden, and mounting two brass 12-pounder cannon on the fort ramparts, “one for the morning and evening gun, and the other to assist in case there should stray into this region someone entitled to a salute.” During the Civil War, Phelps was appointed brigadier general in the 1st Vermont Infantry. An avid abolitionist, Phelps resigned in 1862 in protest over the army’s unwillingness to recruit and use African American troops. The following year, the army reversed its policy and created several black regiments. Phelps retired to his hometown of Brattleboro, Vermont, where he became active in local politics. In 1880 Phelps ran for president of the United States on the Anti-Masonic/American Party ticket. He received 700 votes.

Library of Congress

Engraving of Lieutenant General John C. Pemberton, as commander of the Army of Vicksburg, Army of the Confederacy, ca. 1862

Lieutenant John C. Pemberton

1814–1871

John Clifford Pemberton graduated from West Point in 1837 and was assigned to Fort Mackinac three years later. As he approached his first winter on the island, the young, single, and lonely officer wrote his brother complaining, "I rather despised Detroit when stationed there, but in comparison with this place, it stands forth in bold relief—still I have even here occasional pleasures." Pemberton later served with distinction in the Mexican-American War and, following the war, married Martha Thompson, daughter of a Virginia plantation owner. At the outbreak of the Civil War, Pemberton resigned his commission and joined the Confederate army, where he rose to the rank of lieutenant general. Pemberton was in command of the Confederate army that was defeated at Vicksburg, Mississippi, in the summer of 1863.

Massachusetts Mollus Photograph Collection, U.S. Army Heritage and Education Center, Carlisle, PA

Brigadier General John M. Jones, C.S.A., ca. 1863

Lieutenant John Marshall Jones

1820–1864

John Marshall Jones graduated from West Point in 1841 and was immediately assigned to the 5th Infantry at Fort Mackinac. Jones spent two years at the island fort and left only once, in September 1843, to lead a detachment of soldiers assisting with the Ojibway Indian treaty payments at LaPointe, Wisconsin. A native of Charlottesville, Virginia, Jones resigned his commission in May 1861 and was immediately commissioned captain in the Confederate States Army. Promoted to the rank of brigadier general in May 1863, Jones was killed in action during the Battle of the Wilderness six months later.

Massachusetts Mollus Photograph Collection, U.S. Army Heritage and Education Center, Carlisle, PA

George W. Getty, ca. 1865

Lieutenant George Washington Getty

1819–1901

George W. Getty graduated from West Point in 1840 and served with the 4th Regiment of Artillery at Fort Mackinac one year later. Getty participated in the Mexican-American and the Third Seminole wars. Getty saw extensive combat during the Civil War and was severely wounded at the Battle of the Wilderness in May 1864. He recovered to lead troops during the Siege of Petersburg one month later and served through the final campaign of the Army of the Potomac. In March 1865 he was appointed brevet major general "for gallant and meritorious services in the pursuit of the insurgent army under General R. E. Lee." Getty remained in the army after the war and retired in 1882.

Mackinac State Historic Parks

Lieutenant Henry Whiting, reproduction of an oil painting by Charles Deas, ca. 1841. In the portrait Whiting wears a black band on his left arm, a traditional badge of mourning, presumably to honor president, and former U.S. army general, William Henry Harrison, who died on April 4, 1841. The portrait was painted by Charles Deas in 1841 in St. Louis and likely brought by Whiting to Fort Mackinac in November of that year.

Record Group 98s—Civil War Photos Box 84.62, U.S. Army Heritage and Education Center, Carlisle, PA

Colonel Henry Whiting, Second Vermont Infantry, ca. 1862

Lieutenant Henry Whiting

1818–1887

An 1840 graduate of West Point, Lieutenant Henry Whiting served with the 5th Infantry at Fort Mackinac from 1841 to 1845. While at the island post, Whiting married Pamelia Rice, daughter of Mackinac physician Justin Rice, on November 29, 1843. Refusing to support the looming war with Mexico, Whiting resigned his commission in 1846. Two years later Whiting engaged in the lumber and mercantile business in St. Clair, Michigan, with Willard Parker and his father-in-law, Dr. Justin Rice. Whiting joined the Vermont Volunteers and was commissioned a colonel in the 2nd Regiment at the outbreak of the Civil War. He was engaged in several battles, including Fredericksburg, where he faced Confederate forces led by John Marshall Jones, with whom he served at Fort Mackinac 20 years earlier. Whiting returned to his mercantile business in St. Clair after the war and died there on June 23, 1887.

Massachusetts Mollus Photograph Collection, U.S. Army Heritage and Education Center, Carlisle, PA

Major General George C. Thomas, ca. 1860

Lieutenant George Cummins Thomas

1813–1882

George C. Thomas graduated from West Point in 1836 and stayed in the U.S. Army for only six years before he retired. He served very briefly at Fort Mackinac with the 4th Artillery in the fall of 1841. Following retirement, Thomas worked as an attorney settling land claims in Washington, DC. During the Civil War Thomas served as major general of the Militia of the District of Columbia. He continued in command of the militia until the end of the war, when he became a clerk in the Quartermaster General's office in Washington.

Edward Nicholas

Reverend John O'Brien, from a daguerreotype, ca. 1848

Edward Nicholas

Charlotte O'Brien, from a daguerreotype, ca. 1848

Reverend John O'Brien

ca. 1800–1864

Reverend John O'Brien was appointed U.S. Army chaplain for Fort Mackinac in 1842 and served in this capacity for the next 19 years. Reverend O'Brien was the first, and only, regular army chaplain at Fort Mackinac. He lived with his wife, Charlotte, and sons in the west apartment of the officers' hill quarters, and his post chapel was in the soldiers' barracks. Ordained an Episcopal priest, O'Brien ministered to both soldiers and civilians, and the origin of Mackinac Island's Trinity Episcopal Church, founded in 1873, can be traced to O'Brien's service to the island community. O'Brien's wife, Charlotte, and son Allen both died while at Mackinac and are buried in the post cemetery.

Thomas G. Shaw

"Death of Colonel Martin Scott, at the Battle of Molino Del Rea," published in the *Rough and Ready Almanac*, 1849

Captain Martin Scott

1788–1847

A veteran of the War of 1812, Martin Scott transferred to the 5th Infantry during the army reorganization of 1821 and was promoted to captain in 1828. While in command of Fort Mackinac (1842–1845), Captain Scott made substantial improvements to the post. During an October 1843 inspection tour, Colonel George Croghan credited Scott with "untiring efforts to repair and improve the appearance of his post, which is now in point of order and extreme neatness perhaps without parallel in the country." One year later, Joseph LeConte visited the post and described Scott as "an interesting man, with strong, alert, athletic figure, bright, eager, keen gray eyes, and ruddy face, bronzed by long exposure." Known for his hunting prowess, Scott's apartment in the officers' stone quarters was "adorned with elk-horns and buffalo-heads and grinning jaws of panthers; before every door were rugs of bearskins and buffalo-robes." Upon leaving Fort Mackinac, Scott was engaged in field duty during the Mexican-American War and was killed in action at the Battle of Molino del Rey in 1847.

Opposite: "General Prospect of Fort Mackinaw County Michigan: For the Commanding Capt. Martin Scott," drawn by Private William G. Brenshutz, 1845. This image depicts soldiers from the 5th Regiment of Infantry on the Fort Mackinac parade ground. Captain Scott is presumed to be the officer on the left facing the troops with his right arm extended.

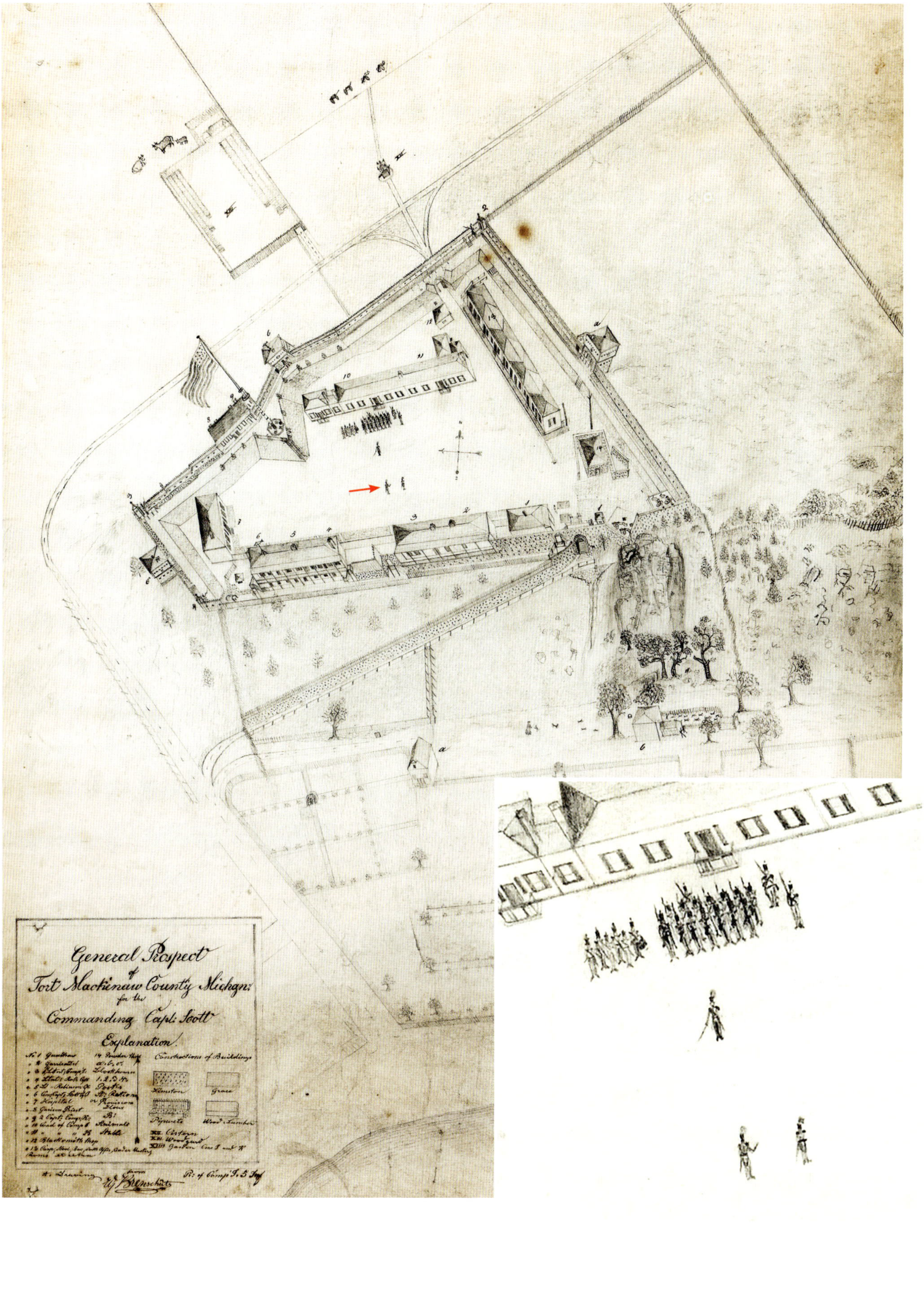

William L. Clements Library, University of Michigan, Ann Arbor

Lieutenant William Root, ca. 1845

Lieutenant William Root

A native of New York state, William Root received a direct commission from civilian life into the 5th Regiment of Infantry in 1837. Root served at Fort Mackinac from 1843 to May 1845 and lived in the east end of the officers' stone quarters. One year later he resigned his commission in the U.S. Army.

Medicalantiques.com, Douglas Arbittier, MD, and the De Gregoris Image Collection

Dr. Levi Holden, ca. 1863

Dr. Levi Holden
1818–1874

Dr. Levi Holden was appointed assistant surgeon in the U.S. Army in June 1840 and was posted to Fort Mackinac in 1843–1844. During the Civil War, Holden served as medical director of the Mountain, Ohio, and Monongahela departments and chief medical purveyor at Chicago. Thereafter, Dr. Holden served on a number of army medical boards prior to his retirement in 1868.

Massachusetts Mollus Photograph Collection, U.S. Army Heritage and Education Center, Carlisle, PA

Major General Frederick Steele, ca. 1864

Lieutenant Frederick Steele

1819–1868

Fort Mackinac was Lieutenant Frederick Steele's first posting after graduating from the U.S. Military Academy in 1843. Steele continued to serve in the 5th Infantry through the Mexican-American War, where he earned two brevet promotions, to first lieutenant for his participation in the Battle of Contreras and to captain for the Battle of Chapultepec. At the outbreak of the Civil War, Steele was appointed colonel in the 8th Iowa Volunteers. He eventually rose to the rank of major general during the war and served as a division, corps, and department commander.

Massachusetts Mollus Photograph Collection, U.S. Army Heritage and Education Center, Carlisle, PA

Brigadier General John C. Robinson, ca. 1863

Lieutenant John C. Robinson

1817–1897

John Cleveland Robinson attended West Point for three years before he was dismissed for insubordination in 1838. After briefly studying law, Robinson was directly commissioned into the army in 1839. He served as a second lieutenant with the 5th Infantry at Fort Mackinac in 1843–1845 and lived in the officers' stone quarters, adjacent to his commanding officer, Captain Martin Scott. Robinson participated in several battles during the Mexican-American War and proved to be a very capable infantry officer during the Civil War. Promoted to brigadier general in 1862, Robinson led Union army divisions at the battles of Chancellorsville, Gettysburg, the Wilderness, and Spotsylvania Court House, where he was shot through the knee, requiring the amputation of his left leg. He retired in 1869 and became active in politics (New York state lieutenant governor, 1872–1874) and veterans' affairs (commander of the Grand Army of the Republic, 1877–1879). Robinson was awarded the Congressional Medal of Honor in 1894 for leading his troops at Spotsylvania.

Dr. Charles Carter Keeney, ca. 1861

Dr. Charles Carter Keeney

1821–1883

Appointed to the Army Medical Department in 1842, Dr. Charles Carter Keeney served as Fort Mackinac's post surgeon for one month in the spring of 1845 when Dr. John Byrne traveled to Sault Ste. Marie to tend to Captain Alexander Johnston, commandant at Fort Brady. While Keeney's service at Mackinac was brief, he had a long career as a military physician with service in the Mexican-American War and Civil War. Dr. Keeney remained in service after the war and was promoted colonel and assistant surgeon general in 1882, one year before he died while on active duty.

Major General Silas Casey, ca. 1862

Massachusetts Mollus Photograph Collection, U.S. Army Heritage and Education Center, Carlisle, PA

Captain Silas Casey

1807–1882

Captain Silas Casey replaced Martin Scott as commandant of Fort Mackinac in September 1845. While at Mackinac, Casey became close friends with post chaplain John O'Brien and his wife Charlotte, who described Casey as "quite determined, but very genial, winking at *little* deviations, but not for a moment giving way to contumacious offenders." In May 1847, Casey and his company were transferred from Mackinac to service in the Mexican-American War, where he saw extensive field duty and was severely wounded at the Battle of Chapultepec. Casey returned to garrison duty following the war and, in 1855, authored the three-volume *System of Infantry Tactics*, which was used by both sides during the Civil War. Casey was promoted to major general during the war and retired from service in 1868.

Captain Morgan L. Gage,
14th Michigan Infantry, ca. 1861

Captain Morgan L. Gage

1807–1876

Regular troops vacated Fort Mackinac in June 1847 to participate in the Mexican Campaign. During their absence, the fort was manned by a company of the 1st Regiment of Michigan Volunteers, Brady Guard, under the command of Captain Morgan L. Gage. After his service at Mackinac, Gage returned to civilian life and later was instrumental in the construction of plank roads in Michigan's Saginaw and Tuscola Counties. Gage was appointed captain in the 14th Michigan Infantry at the beginning of the Civil War, but resigned due to health reasons in 1862.

Library of Congress, Prints & Photographs Division, Civil War Photographs, LC-DIG-cwpb-05983

Brigadier General William N. R. Beall, C.S.A., ca. 1862

Lieutenant William Nelson Rector Beall

1825–1883

William N. R. Beall graduated from West Point in 1848 and spent his first year of service as a brevet second lieutenant with the 4th Infantry at Fort Mackinac. Beall was later promoted and appointed to one of the new cavalry regiments in 1855. Six years later, at the outbreak of the Civil War, the Arkansas-raised Beall resigned his commission and joined the Confederate States Army as a cavalry officer. Beall surrendered his command and was taken prisoner at the Siege of Port Hudson (Louisiana) on July 8, 1863. Beall was released on parole in early 1864 and sent by the Confederate government to New York City, where he served as the Confederacy's agent for prisoner exchange.

Will Dunniway

Lieutenant Hiram Dryer

1822–1867

Hiram Dryer's military service began in 1846 when he enlisted in the Regiment of Mounted Rifles. Soon after, his company was posted to Mexico, where he was promoted to first sergeant and participated in the campaign against Mexico City. Dryer received a battlefield commission as second lieutenant for his service during the war and was transferred to the 4th Regiment of Infantry. Lieutenant Dryer was with the first troops that reoccupied Fort Mackinac after the Mexican-American War in November 1848. He served nearly four years at Mackinac with brief stints as commanding officer in 1849 and 1850. Dryer remained with the 4th Infantry throughout the Civil War and was cited for "gallant and meritorious service" in the battles of Fredericksburg and Chancellorsville. Dryer died of pneumonia while commanding Fort Randell, South Dakota, in 1867.

Lieutenant Hiram Dryer, ca. 1861

Ordnance Sergeant William David Marshall

1800–1884

William Marshall was Fort Mackinac's oldest and longest-serving soldier. Marshall joined the army in 1823 and came to Fort Mackinac 25 years later as post ordnance sergeant. The "Old Sergeant," as he was known to all in his later years, was caretaker of Fort Mackinac when it was abandoned during the Third Seminole War (1856–1858) and the Civil War. In 1871 Captain Leslie Smith, citing Marshal's "singularly long and faithful term of service," requested a promotion for the 71-year-old sergeant so that his remaining years might be "passed in ease and comfort which he so well deserves." The army denied Smith's request, and Marshal continued to serve at Fort Mackinac until his death in 1884, one year before the army retirement program was enacted.

Watercolor portrait of Ordnance Sergeant William D. Marshall based on a description by his grandson Chester Marshall, by Ellen Parker Beard, 1997

Captain Joseph B. Brown with four-year-old son Warren, 1858

Courtesy Archives of Michigan

Roger Hunt Collection, U.S. Army Heritage and Education Center, Carlisle, PA

Brevet Brigadier General Joseph B. Brown, ca. 1866

Dr. Joseph Bullock Brown

1822–1891

Joseph Bullock Brown was appointed as an assistant surgeon in the U.S. Army Medical Corps in June 1849 and assigned to Fort Mackinac one month later. Dr. Brown served the island fort for one year during his first posting and returned for a second stint in 1854–1855. While at Mackinac, Brown cared for Charlotte O'Brien, wife of his good friend post chaplain Rev. John O'Brien, during her unsuccessful battle with tuberculosis. Despite having "the highest opinion of Dr. Brown and his care and assiduity and skill in meeting the various symptoms," Mrs. O'Brien succumbed to the disease on March 17, 1855. During the Civil War, Dr. Brown was assigned to the 4th Army Corps/ Army of the Potomac which included field service throughout the entire Peninsula Campaign. He was later made chief officer in the surgeon general's office in the Army of the Cumberland. Brown was promoted to brevet brigadier general in 1866 and retired from the army as an assistant surgeon general in 1886.

Courtesy U.S. National Library of Medicine

Dr. Charles H. Laub, ca. 1860

Dr. Charles H. Laub

1805–1876

Dr. Charles Laub was appointed lieutenant and assistant surgeon on November 30, 1836. Laub was promoted to captain in 1841 and posted to Fort Mackinac from August 1850 through June 1852. At the time, the Medical Department required post surgeons to complete and submit detailed meteorological reports on the 21st of the month, four times a year. On these days Dr. Laub recorded hourly readings for temperature, wind, clouds, "clearness of sky," and general comments. Laub was promoted brevet lieutenant colonel and medical inspector for "faithful and meritorious service" during the Civil War. Dr. Laub remained in the army after the war and, in 1876, was appointed assistant medical purveyor.

Massachusetts Mollus Photograph Collection, U.S. Army Heritage and Education Center, Carlisle, PA

Lieutenant David A. Russell

1820–1864

David Allen Russell graduated from West Point in 1845 and, two years later, led troops in several engagements during the Mexican-American War. Russell came to Fort Mackinac with Company H, 4th Infantry, in November 1850 and served as post commander before being replaced by Captain Charles Larnard the following June. Russell joined the Massachusetts Volunteers during the Civil War and was promoted to brigadier general in 1862. He fought in several battles, including the Peninsula Campaign, Antietam, and Fredericksburg, before he was mortally wounded by a shell fragment during the Battle of Opequon on September 19, 1864. Fort D. A. Russell in the Wyoming Territory was named in his honor.

Brigadier General David A. Russell, ca. 1863

Mackinac State Historic Parks, Acc. No. 2008.00.226

Major Thomas Williams, ca. 1861

Captain Thomas Williams

1815–1862

Thomas William's grandfather (Thomas Williams, 1744–1785) moved to Detroit while it was still under British rule. His marriage to Cecile Campeau was performed by Colonel Arent S. DePeyster (former commandant at Michilimackinac), who also baptized his son, John R. Williams, the following year. John was elected mayor of Detroit in 1824, and John R Street was subsequently named in his honor. His son, Captain Thomas Williams, an 1837 graduate of West Point, commanded Fort Mackinac from 1852 to 1856. Williams oversaw multiple improvements to the fort during his tenure, including construction of a new soldiers' barracks following a devastating fire in January 1855. While at Mackinac, Williams married Mary Neosho Bailey, daughter of post surgeon Dr. Joseph Bailey who lived in the adjoining apartment at the officers' stone quarters. Williams was promoted to brigadier general of volunteers in 1861 and killed in action during the Battle of Baton Rouge one year later.

Mackinac State Historic Parks, Acc. No. 1998.23.4

View of the Town of Mackinac, 1855

View of the town of Mackinac, colored engraving originally published as a black-and-white image in *Ballou's Pictorial Drawing-Room Companion,* May 5, 1885. Based on a sketch made by an unnamed U.S. officer, this is likely the work of post commandant Major Thomas Williams. The engraving shows the fort as it appeared in the 1850s, a quiet time in Mackinac's history between the heyday of the fur trade and the advent of tourism following the Civil War.

Courtesy Nate Maas

George W. Rains, ca. 1890

Lieutenant George W. Rains

1817–1898

George Washington Rains was born in North Carolina in 1817 and graduated from West Point, third in his class, in 1842. Rains fought in the Mexican-American War and was cited for "gallant and meritorious conduct" in the battles of Contreras, Churubusco, and Chapultepec. Following the war, Rains was stationed on garrison duty at several posts, including Fort Mackinac in 1852–1854. Rains resigned his commission in 1856 to run the Washington Iron Works in New Jersey. At the outbreak of the Civil War, Rains joined the Confederate army and was commissioned a major. Assigned the task of supplying gunpowder to the Confederate army, Rains established the government powder mills at Augusta, Georgia.

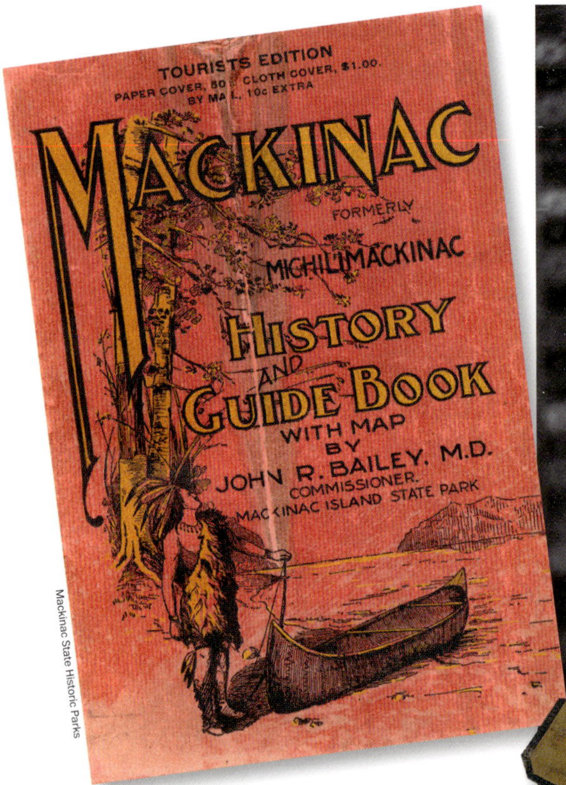

Mackinac State Historic Parks

Mackinac, Formerly Michilimackinac, History and Guide Book with Map, by John R. Bailey. Bailey's guidebook, filled with historical information, photographs, and an island map, was first published in 1895 and reprinted several times.

Mackinac State Historic Parks

Dr. John R. Bailey, ca. 1900

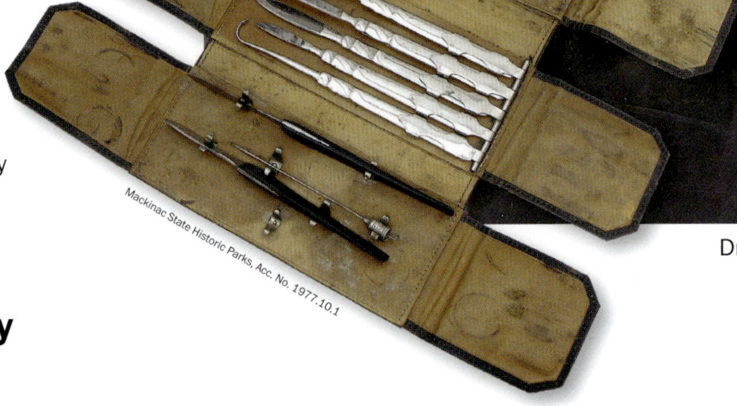

Mackinac State Historic Parks, Acc. No. 1977.10.1

Dr. John R. Bailey's U.S. Army medical kit, ca. 1890

Dr. John R. Bailey

1833–1910

John Reed Bailey was born in New York City, the eldest son of Dr. Joseph Bailey, who served as post surgeon at Fort Mackinac from 1852 to 1854. Bailey graduated from the University of Michigan Medical School in 1854 and immediately moved to Mackinac Island, where he began a private practice and an association with Fort Mackinac that lasted for more than 50 years. Bailey served as a contract physician to the garrison at Fort Mackinac multiple times when army surgeons were not available between 1854, when he replaced his father, to 1895, when he was the fort's last doctor. Dr. Bailey left the island during the Civil War when he joined the 8th Missouri Infantry Volunteers as a surgeon. Returning to the island after the war, Bailey became active in veteran's organizations and wrote several papers and books on Mackinac history. Bailey served on the Mackinac Island State Park Commission, the agency tasked with preserving Fort Mackinac, from 1903 to 1909.

Massachusetts Mollus Photograph Collection, U.S. Army Heritage and Education Center, Carlisle, PA

Captain William Terrill, ca. 1861

Lieutenant William Terrill

1834–1862

An 1853 graduate of West Point, William Rufus Terrill joined Company L, 4th Artillery at Fort Mackinac on September 18, 1856. One month later, Terrill and the rest of his company vacated the island fort and traveled to Fort Myers, Florida to take part in the Third Seminole War. At the outbreak of the Civil War, the Virginia-born Terrill confirmed his allegiance to the United States when he telegraphed the War Department saying, "I am now and ever will be true to my oath and my country." One year later, Terrill was killed in action leading his artillery brigade against Confederate forces at the Battle of Perryville, Kentucky.

Library of Congress

Major General Arnold Elzey, ca. 1863

Captain Arnold Elzey

1816–1871

Arnold Elzey was born at this father's plantation "Elmwood" in Somerset County, Maryland, in 1816. An 1837 graduate of West Point, Captain Elzey commanded Fort Mackinac during the summer of 1857. Sympathetic to the secessionist cause, Elzey resigned his commission on April 25, 1861, just 11 days after the surrender of Fort Sumter. He organized the 1st Maryland Infantry and was appointed brigadier general in the summer of 1861. Elzey was severely wounded in the face during the Seven Days Battles but remained in service through the end of the war.

Massachusetts Mollus Photograph Collection, U.S. Army Heritage and Education Center, Carlisle, PA

"Officers of the 1st Brigade/Horse Artillery, near Fair Oaks, Virginia, June 1862." Captain Henry Benson is standing, top row, third from the left.

Lieutenant Henry Benson

1824–1862

Henry Benson enlisted as a private in the 2nd Regiment of Artillery in 1845 and served in the Mexican-American War, reaching the rank of first sergeant before he was discharged in 1848. One year later, Benson secured an officer's commission and was stationed briefly at Fort Mackinac during the summer of 1857. Promoted to his captaincy in 1862, Benson served as a Union artillery officer during the Civil War before he died of wounds received during the Battle of Malvern Hill, Virginia, on August 11, 1862.

U.S. Army Heritage and Education Center, R.G. 5265, NYSAG.8, Carlisle, PA

Lieutenant Guilford D. Bailey

1834–1862

New York state native Guilford Dudley Bailey graduated from West Point in 1856 and served briefly at Fort Mackinac the following summer. Four years later, during the Civil War, Bailey was commissioned colonel in the New York Volunteer Light Artillery and named chief of artillery for General Silas Casey's Third Division of the IV Corps. He led Casey's artillery through the May 1862 Peninsular Campaign, and was killed in action on May 31, 1862, at the Battle of Fair Oaks. Following the battle, General Casey, who commanded Fort Mackinac in 1845, noted, "I cannot forebear mention of the severe misfortune suffered by the division and the service in the loss of Colonel G. D. Bailey, my chief of artillery. . . . Col Bailey was an officer of thorough military education; of clear and accurate mind; cool, determined, and intrepid in the discharge of his duty, and promising with riper years to honor still more the profession to which he was devoted."

Lieutenant Colonel Guilford D. Bailey, New York Volunteer Light Infantry, ca. 1862

Dr. John F. Head, major, Medical Department, U.S. Army, ca. 1863

Massachusetts Mollus Photograph Collection, U.S. Army Heritage and Education Center, Carlisle, PA

Dr. John Frazier Head

1821–1908

Massachusetts-born John Frazier Head was appointed to the U.S. Army Medical Department in August 1846 and immediately assigned to service in the Mexican-American War. Dr. Head participated in several campaigns including the Siege of Vera Cruz and the battles of Contreras and Churubusco. Following the war, Head served as assistant surgeon at several posts, including Fort Mackinac in 1858–1859. While at Mackinac, Dr. Head drafted plans for a new two-story hospital that was eventually constructed in 1860–1861. During the Civil War, Dr. Head was post surgeon at the U.S. Military Academy at West Point and remained in this position until 1868. Head remained in the army until 1885 and retired as a colonel and assistant surgeon general.

Lieutenant Henry A. Smalley

1834–1888

An 1854 graduate of West Point, Henry Adams Smalley served at several posts across the country before being transferred to Fort Mackinac with Company G, 2nd Artillery, in July 1858. Just three months later, Smalley left the post on leave for six months followed by detached duty at Plattsburg Barracks in New York. Returning in June 1860, Smalley remained at the post until his company was ordered to Washington, DC, to protect the capitol at the outbreak of the Civil War. In September 1861 he was commissioned colonel in the 5th Vermont Volunteers and led his regiment in the Peninsula Campaign in Virginia. It was during this engagement that he contracted malaria and was forced to resign his commission in the volunteers. Returning to the regular army, Smalley served in several noncombat roles until the end of the war, when he resigned. Smalley became a successful businessman, serving as president of the Nova Scotia Quarrying Company and publishing newspapers.

Colonel Henry A. Smalley, 5th Vermont Volunteers, ca. 1862

Massachusetts Mollus Photograph Collection, U.S. Army Heritage and Education Center, Carlisle, PA

Surgeon General William A. Hammond, ca. 1864

Massachusetts Mollus Photograph Collection, U.S. Army Heritage and Education Center, Carlisle, PA

Dr. William Alexander Hammond
1828–1900

Born in Maryland, William Hammond entered the army as an assistant surgeon in 1849. He served at West Point and at posts throughout the west, including Fort Mackinac from October 1859 to September 1860. While at Mackinac, Hammond toiled away in the dilapidated 1828 hospital while awaiting funds to construct a new building designed by his predecessor, Dr. John Frazier Head. Hammond resigned his commission two months after leaving Mackinac to accept the chair of anatomy and physiology in the medical school at the University of Maryland in Baltimore. During the Civil War Hammond was appointed surgeon general, the army's highest-ranking medical officer. Dr. Hammond reorganized the medical department that quickly grew from serving a small peacetime establishment to a vast army with over 500,000 soldiers.

Major General George L. Hartsuff, ca. 1863

Lieutenant George Lucas Hartsuff

1830–1874

George L. Hartsuff moved to Michigan from New York with his family when he was 12 years old. Hartsuff graduated from West Point in 1852 and fought in the Third Seminole War, where he was wounded twice in action near Fort Myers, Florida, in 1856. After a brief stint at West Point as an assistant professor of artillery tactics, Lieutenant Hartsuff transferred to Fort Mackinac in July 1859. During his 13 months at Mackinac, Hartsuff was in charge of the fort's commissary and quartermaster supplies. Promoted to brigadier general, U.S. Volunteers, during the Civil War, Hartsuff was severely wounded in the hip while leading troops at Antietam. President Lincoln visited Hartsuff while he was recovering in the nearby field hospital, and promoted him to major general two months later. Hartsuff subsequently died in 1874 due to complications from his battle wounds. Two U.S. Army forts were named in Hartsuff's honor, one in Florida (1856) and another in Nebraska (1874).

Courtesy U.S. National Library of Medicine

Dr. Albert Hartsuff, ca. 1880

Dr. Albert Hartsuff

1837–1908

Dr. Albert Hartsuff worked as a civilian physician (acting assistant surgeon) at Fort Mackinac for six weeks in the fall of 1860. He was undoubtedly drawn to Mackinac by his brother, Lieutenant George Hartsuff, who served with the 2nd Artillery at the island post. Dr. Hartsuff found military service to his liking and joined the U.S. Army Medical Department one year later. Hartsuff remained in the army after the Civil War and was eventually promoted to the rank of colonel, deputy surgeon general, in 1900. He retired as brigadier general the following year.

Courtesy U.S. National Library of Medicine

Dr. George Cooper, ca. 1865

Dr. George E. Cooper

Pennsylvania native George E. Cooper joined the army medical service in 1847 and was soon assigned to field duty in the Mexican-American War. Following the war, Cooper served as an assistant surgeon at numerous stations and arrived at Fort Mackinac in October 1860. Cooper was the first surgeon to enjoy the benefits of Fort Mackinac's new hospital constructed in 1860–1861. Cooper left Mackinac when the post was vacated during the Civil War and was promoted to surgeon and served in several administrative posts, including medical purveyor in Philadelphia, special inspector in the Office of the Assistant Surgeon General, and medical director for the Army of the Cumberland and Military Division of Tennessee.

Fort Mackinac post hospital, ca. 1885

Fort Mackinac Post Hospital

The two-story main section of Fort Mackinac's new post hospital, constructed in 1860–1861, included spaces for a storeroom, office and dispensary, steward's and matron's quarters, and ward rooms. The antenna-like objects on the roof supported the telegraph wire that connected the hospital with the island telegraph station that was installed in 1883.

U.S. SOLDIERS AT MACKINAC, 1862–1895

Massachusetts Mollus Photograph Collection, U.S. Army Heritage and Education Center, Carlisle, PA

Colonel Grover S. Wormer, 30th Michigan Infantry, ca. 1864

Captain Grover S. Wormer

1821–1904

Grover Salmon Wormer commanded the "Stanton Guard," a Michigan volunteer infantry unit tasked with overseeing the incarceration of three influential Tennessee civilians at Fort Mackinac during the Civil War. Arrested by Union General Andrew Johnson for "treasonous inclinations," the prisoners were transferred to the island fort in May 1862. Described by prisoner Josephus Conn Guild as "a gentleman who did honor to the uniform he wore," Wormer treated the Confederate sympathizers with respect and permitted daily walks along the island's roads and trails attended by armed guards. The prisoners were removed from Fort Mackinac in late September 1862 and the Stanton Guard was soon disbanded. One month later, Wormer joined the 8th Michigan Volunteer Cavalry and was eventually promoted to brevet brigadier general.

Richard K. Tibbals Collection, U.S. Army Heritage and Education Center, Carlisle, PA

Lieutenant Washington L. Wood, 19th Illinois Volunteer Infantry, ca. 1862

Lieutenant Washington L. Wood

Washington Wood was commissioned first lieutenant in Company C, 19th Regiment, Illinois Volunteer Infantry, on September 6, 1862. Four months later Wood was severely wounded during the Battle of Stones River, Tennessee. Wood resigned his commission in the volunteers in December 1863 but was appointed second lieutenant in the Veteran Reserve Corps, a unit composed of soldiers wounded during the war but still capable of limited garrison duties, in October 1864. Wood served with the 4th Independent Company, Veteran Reserve Corps, that temporarily occupied Fort Mackinac after the Civil War during the summer of 1866.

Fort Mackinac during the Civil War, Summer 1862

Mackinac State Historic Parks, Acc. No. 2009.93.2

Stanton Guard soldiers on duty at the South Sally Port

Clarke Historical Library, Central Michigan University

Above: South elevation of Fort Mackinac, revealing the dilapidated condition of the fort in the 1860s. This photograph shows that a portion of the collapsed stone retaining wall has been temporarily replaced with wooden pickets.

Right: Soldiers in dress uniforms assembled on the fort parade ground. In the foreground is the powder magazine, built by the British in 1780–1781 and torn down in 1878 to make space for construction of the post commissary.

Mackinac State Historic Parks, Acc. No. 1997.00.393

Diane Rouse

Julius Stommel, ca. 1864

Lieutenant Julius Stommel

1828–1891

A native of Brohl, East Prussia, Julius Strommel joined the 41st New York Volunteer Infantry as a private in 1861 and was commissioned second lieutenant in June 1863. One month later, Stommel was severely wounded at the Battle of Gettysburg and eventually transferred to the Veteran Reserve Corps. Stommel arrived at Fort Mackinac in August 1867 as a lieutenant in the 43rd Regiment of Infantry, which was created after the Civil War with former members of the Veteran Reserve Corps. Stommel remained at the post until he was transferred to Fort Wayne (Detroit) in May 1869.

City of Mackinac Island

William P. Preston, ca. 1900

Sergeant William Paul Preston

1845–1915

William P. Preston served with the 4th Delaware Volunteers during the Civil War. Preston participated in most of the battles of the Army of the Potomac and was present at Appomattox when General Robert E. Lee surrendered to General Ulysses S. Grant. Preston joined the regular army following the war and arrived at Fort Mackinac as first sergeant with the 43rd Regiment of Infantry in August 1867. In May 1869 Preston received a disability discharge and, a few weeks later, married Mary Ann Overall, daughter of island saloon keeper Henry Overall. Mary Ann died four years later, and, in 1875, Preston married Mary Ann's younger sister Kate. Preston operated Preston's Empire Saloon on Main Street and became involved in local politics, serving as president of the village and mayor of the City of Mackinac Island for 17 years.

Mackinac State Historic Parks

Captain Leslie Smith, photographed during his service at Fort Mackinac, 1869–1874

Captain Leslie Smith

1825–1907

Born in Ireland in 1825, Leslie Smith immigrated to the United States and enlisted in the army in 1849. He served as a private, corporal, and sergeant during his five-year enlistment. At the outbreak of the Civil War, Smith was commissioned second lieutenant in the 1st U.S. Infantry and spent the war on administrative duties with the Subsistence Department. Smith remained with the 1st Infantry after the war and commanded Fort Mackinac from 1869 to 1874. In 1872 Captain Smith joined with local residents to form an Episcopal Church congregation on Mackinac Island, and he refitted the fort chapel for their use. Smith was elected senior warden and his wife, Louisa, joined post surgeon Dr. Samuel Jessop as a member of the choir.

Mackinac State Historic Parks

Mrs. Leslie (Louisa) Smith, ca. 1869–1874

Mackinac State Historic Parks

Dr. Samuel Jessop, ca. 1890

Dr. Samuel S. Jessop

1835–1892

Samuel S. Jessop was born in Ireland in 1835. He studied medicine in New York after immigrating to the United States and was commissioned second lieutenant, assistant surgeon, in the U.S. Volunteers during the Civil War. Jessop was appointed to the Medical Department following the war and assigned to Fort Mackinac in 1870–1872. Six years later, Jessop resigned his commission and returned to Mackinac Island, where he opened a private medical practice. Jessop died in 1892 and is buried in the island's Protestant Cemetery.

Mackinac State Historic Parks

Major (Retired) Thomas Sharpe, ca. 1900

Lieutenant Thomas Sharpe

1838–1917

Thomas Sharpe began his military career when he joined the 7th Pennsylvania Volunteers as a private in 1861. Two years later, he was commissioned captain in the 65th U.S. Colored Infantry, a position he held until the end of the Civil War. In 1870 he was assigned to the 1st Regiment of Infantry and arrived at Fort Mackinac on May 27, 1871. While at Mackinac, Sharpe met and married Helen Rice, daughter of island merchant James Rice. After the service at Ste. Anne's Church, the wedding party proceeded to the Rice residence, where "music and dancing prevailed and all went 'Merry as a marriage bell' from the tying of the knot to the good-bye at midnight." Sharpe remained at Fort Mackinac until July 1874 and commanded the post during his final two months. Sharpe retired from the army as a major in 1898.

Medicalantiques.com, Douglas Arbittier, MD, and the De Gregoris Image Collection

Dr. William M. Notson

1836–1882

William Monroe Notson attended the Pennsylvania College of Physicians and Surgeons and was commissioned first lieutenant and assistant surgeon in the U.S. Army in April 1862. Dr. Notson served with the Army of the Potomac in 1862–1863 and completed his Civil War service on general hospital duties in Washington, DC. Promoted to captain in 1868, Notson arrived at Fort Mackinac on August 12, 1872, and soon developed a prickly relationship with post commander Captain Leslie Smith. Smith accused the doctor of spending too much time at the Mission House and in a "low grog shop" in the village, while Notson charged the commandant with misusing government property for his own benefit. Notson was transferred to Fort Gratiot after a little more than one year at the island fort.

Dr. William M. Notson, ca. 1862

Dr. Carlos Carvallo, ca. 1868

Courtesy U.S. National Library of Medicine

Dr. Carlos Carvallo

d. 1882

Born in Santiago, Chile, Carlos Carvallo was appointed to the U.S. Army Medical Corps in 1867. Dr. Carvallo replaced post surgeon William Notson at Fort Mackinac in September 1873 and soon experienced similar challenges working with Captain Leslie Smith. Concerned about the health of soldiers incarcerated in the post guardhouse, Carvallo petitioned the commandant to improve ventilation by adding a window to the cell room. Smith rejected Carvallo's request, responding that, if anything, the cell should be made less comfortable so that the men would "not be so anxious to get in confinement." Like his predecessor, Dr. Carvallo remained at Fort Mackinac for only one year.

Captain Charles J. Dickey, ca. 1875

Andrew Burt Collection, U.S. Army Heritage and Education Center, Carlisle, PA

Captain Charles J. Dickey

1837–1893

Charles John Dickey was appointed first lieutenant in the 13th U.S. Infantry at the outbreak of the Civil War. He fought in multiple campaigns and battles throughout the war and was promoted twice for "gallant and meritorious service." Dickey commanded Fort Mackinac in 1874–1875 and remained as a company commander at Mackinac for another year after that. On July 9, 1876, just two weeks after General George A. Custer's defeat at the Little Bighorn, Dickey received telegraphic orders to proceed with his company from Fort Mackinac to Fort Abraham Lincoln, Dakota Territory, to join General Alfred Terry's Sioux Campaign. After a year in the field, Dickey returned to Fort Mackinac but was suspended from duty on October 31, 1877, by general court-martial for being drunk and incapable of performing duties while in Chicago a few months earlier. Dickey remained at the island fort during his suspension, and his commission was restored in October 1878. Dickey retired from the U.S. Army in 1888 as a major.

John McAdam Webster, ca. 1900

Rose Van Allen Webster, ca. 1900

Captain John McAdam Webster

1849–1921

John McAdam Webster was commissioned second lieutenant in the 197th Ohio Volunteers in April 1865, but mustered out just two months later at the end of the Civil War. Finding the military to his liking, Webster attended West Point and graduated in 1871. He served at Fort Mackinac from 1874 to 1879, except during July 1876 to October 1877, when he participated in the Sioux Campaign. While at Mackinac, Webster married Rose Van Allen, whose father owned and operated the Island House hotel. Webster retired from the army in 1898 and later served in the Department of Interior as superintendent at the Colville (Washington) Indian Agency and Spokane Reservation. Webster returned to Mackinac in 1914 and, with Rose, operated the Island House until his death in 1921. Webster is the great uncle of William H. Webster, who served as director of the U.S. Federal Bureau of Investigation from 1978 to 1987, and director of the Central Intelligence Agency from 1987 to 1991.

Courtesy U.S. National Library of Medicine

First Lieutenant and Assistant Surgeon J. V. De Hanne, ca. 1865

Dr. Jean V. De Hanne

1834–1904

Jean Victor De Hanne enlisted as a private in the New York Volunteer Infantry in 1862. He was honorably discharged one year later and attended the New York College of Physicians and Surgeons prior to his appointment as first lieutenant and assistant surgeon in 1864. Following the Civil War, De Hanne was appointed to the regular army and served at Fort Mackinac from 1874 to 1876. Like his medical predecessors, De Hanne struggled to improve the health and sanitary conditions of Fort Mackinac. He made recommendations about locations for sewers and privy pits, the disposal of ashes, manure, and garbage, the condition of uniforms, and the quality of food preparation. Frustrated by the indifference of post commanders, De Hanne remarked that it was not "the custom of this post" to solicit the opinion of the medical officer on such matters.

Nelson Collection, U.S. Army Heritage and Education Center, Carlisle, PA

Major Alfred L. Hough

1826–1908

Alfred Lacey Hough served briefly as an enlisted man at the outbreak of the Civil War before he was commissioned captain in the 19th U.S. Infantry in May 1861. Hough was active in the field during the war and was promoted brevet colonel at the end of the war for his "gallant and meritorious services." Hough commanded Fort Mackinac when Mackinac National Park was created in 1875 and was appointed the park's first superintendent. Hough assisted in drafting the park's rules and regulations, which included language protecting the island's "natural curiosities," one of the first formal efforts to preserve Mackinac Island's unique resources.

Captain Alfred L. Hough, ca. 1863

Mackinac State Historic Parks, Truscott Collection

Captain Charles Augustus Webb, 1877

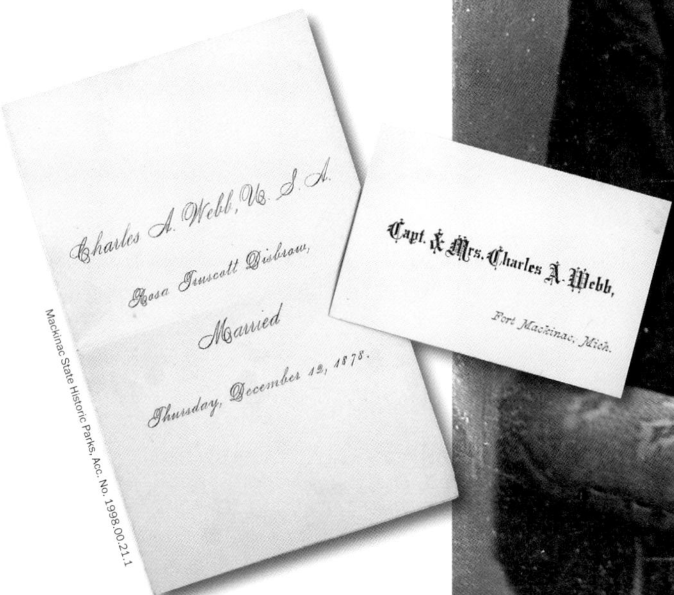

Mackinac State Historic Parks, Acc. No. 1998.00.21.1

Charles and Rosa Webb marriage announcement and calling card

Captain Charles Augustus Webb

1839–1882

Charles Webb's military service began when he was commissioned first lieutenant in the Vermont Volunteers at the outbreak of the Civil War. He mustered out three months later to accept a commission as a captain in the regular army. Webb served the Union army throughout the Civil War and was promoted to brevet major for "gallant and meritorious services during the siege of Vicksburg." In 1877 Webb was convicted of neglect of duty by a general court-martial and arrived at Fort Mackinac in November under arrest and confined to the limits of the post. Three months later he was released from arrest and returned to active duty in charge of Company D, 22nd Infantry. While at Mackinac, Webb married Rosa Truscott Disbrow. After Webb's death from pneumonia at Fort McKavett, Texas, in 1882, Rosa returned to Mackinac, where she established the island's first public library and founded Michigan's first Girl Scout troop.

John Green Ballance, photographed as a cadet at West Point, ca. 1875

Lieutenant John Green Ballance

1853–1910

Illinois native John G. Ballance graduated from West Point in 1875 and was stationed at Fort Mackinac with the 22nd Regiment of Infantry two years later. After leaving Mackinac in 1879, Ballance saw extensive duty in multiple forts around the country, fought in the Ghost Dance War of 1890–1891, and served as judge advocate of the Department of Texas. As a battalion commander during the Philippine-American War, he was involved in 25 separate battles and skirmishes. Balance retired as a lieutenant colonel in 1904 and died six years later.

Courtesy U.S. National Library of Medicine

Dr. Peter Moffatt, ca. 1870

Dr. Peter Moffatt

ca. 1845–1882

Canadian-born Peter Moffatt was commissioned first lieutenant and assistant surgeon in the U.S. Army in October 1867. Dr. Moffatt served as Fort Mackinac's post surgeon from June 1877 to May 1879. Moffatt witnessed the growing popularity of Mackinac as a summer resort destination during his assignment at the island fort. In particular, he noted that those suffering from hay fever "experience almost complete immunity from that troublesome ailment while residing upon the island."

Courtesy of Special Collections and Archives, Wright State University

Oscar D. Ladley, ca. 1878

Lieutenant Oscar D. Ladley

1837–1880

Oscar Derostus Ladley served in the Ohio Volunteer Infantry during the Civil War, beginning as a private in 1861, and mustered out as a captain in 1865. Two years later, Ladley received a commission in the regular army. Ladley was assigned to the 22nd Infantry and arrived at Fort Mackinac with his wife, Clementine, and infant daughter in August 1878. Ladley was delighted to be on "the celebrated Isle of Mackinac" and remarked that he was pleased with his "good quarters with seven rooms, more really than we need."

Mackinac State Historic Parks

Dwight H. Kelton

Lieutenant Dwight H. Kelton

1843–1906

Dwight H. Kelton was born in Montpelier, Vermont, in 1843 and entered military service during the Civil War. He served briefly as a private in the 98th New York Infantry before receiving a captain's commission in the 115th Colored Troops in 1864. Following the war, Kelton was commissioned second lieutenant in the regular army and arrived at Fort Mackinac in 1879 with the 10th Infantry. Three years later, Kelton published *Annals of Fort Mackinac*, a compilation of Mackinac-area historical events, Indian legends, and tourist information that he wrote in his spare time. A vain and self-glorifying author, Kelton extolled his accomplishments at the fort and even renamed Sugar Loaf Rock "Kelton's Pyramid" in later editions. Kelton's tireless efforts to promote and sell his book incurred the wrath of his commanding officer, Captain Edwin Sellers, who ordered him to stop selling the book in the fort and national park. While at Mackinac, Kelton courted Anna Donnelly, daughter of island fisherman Thomas Donnelly and Bridget O'Malley. Kelton retired from the service in 1887 and married Anna in Milwaukee the following year.

Edward H. Plummer, ca. 1898

Edward H. Plummer Collection, U.S. Army Heritage and Education Center, Carlisle, PA

Candlesticks and clock that were wedding gifts and used in the Plummer residence at Fort Mackinac's officers' stone quarters, 1880–1884

Mackinac State Historic Parks, Acc. Nos. 2010.37.1, 2, & 3

Lieutenant Edward H. Plummer

1855–1927

Edward Hinkley Plummer graduated from West Point in 1877 was stationed with the 10th Infantry at Fort Mackinac two years later. During his five-year stay at Fort Mackinac Plummer lived in the east apartment of the officers' stone quarters and was assigned a number of administrative duties, including post adjutant, treasurer, ordnance officer, and signal officer. Plummer was granted a leave of absence in October 1880, when he traveled to Joliet, Illinois, to marry Georgia Moody. After Mackinac, Plummer served at several posts across the country and was active in the Spanish-American War and the Philippine-American War. Plummer was stationed in France during World War I, where he reported on the living and fighting conditions on the front lines. He retired in 1918 as a brigadier general after more than 40 years of service.

Massachusetts Mollus Photograph Collection, U.S. Army Heritage and Education Center, Carlisle, PA

Edwin E. Sellers, ca. 1865

Mackinac State Historic Parks

Edwin E. Sellers and son, Paulding Foote Sellers, ca. 1873

Captain Edwin Elias Sellers

1840–1884

Edwin E. Sellers was commissioned second lieutenant, 10th Infantry, in October 1861 during the Civil War. Sellers was engaged in multiple battles, including Bull Run, Antietam, Fredericksburg, and Gettysburg, and received three brevet promotions for "gallant and meritorious service" during the war. Captain Sellers took command of Fort Mackinac in May 1879 and lived with his wife, Olive, and four sons in the commanding officer's house west of the fort. In 1883 Sellers instituted Decoration Day (now known as Memorial Day) at Fort Mackinac when he suspended regular duty and paraded his soldiers to the post cemetery, where they swept the grounds and decorated the graves of former Union soldiers. Ironically, one year later Sellers was buried in the same cemetery after a brief and sudden bout of pneumonia. Sellers's son David graduated from the U.S. Naval Academy in 1894 and was eventually promoted to admiral and commander-in-chief of the U.S. Fleet in 1933–1934.

Major Walter T. Duggan, ca. 1900

Mackinac State Historic Parks

Lieutenant Walter T. Duggan

1843–1915

Walter Teeling Duggan was born on the Isle of Man, United Kingdom, in 1843 and immigrated with his family to Milwaukee when he was seven years old. Duggan enlisted as a private with the Fifth Wisconsin Volunteers at the beginning of the Civil War and, two years later, accepted a warrant as a hospital steward in the regular army. In 1867 Duggan received a commission as second lieutenant in the 10th U.S. Infantry and was posted to Fort Mackinac from 1879 to 1884. Duggan enlisted eight recruits to fill vacancies in the 10th Infantry while serving as the fort's recruiting officer in 1883. This diverse group included two Canadians, one Russian, one Swede, one Norwegian, and three Americans. Two years after leaving Mackinac, Duggan married Olive, the widow of his former Fort Mackinac commander Captain Edwin Sellers. Duggan received regular promotions throughout his career and retired as a brigadier general in 1907.

Dr. George William Adair, ca. 1880

Courtesy U.S. National Library of Medicine

Dr. George William Adair

1848–1931

Dr. George W. Adair was appointed a lieutenant in the U.S. Army Medical Department in 1874. After serving at several western posts, Adair was transferred to Fort Mackinac, where he was stationed from 1879 to 1881. Adair lived with his wife, Margaret, and two young children, in the new officers' duplex constructed in 1876 when the fort was expanded after the creation of Mackinac National Park. Like his predecessors, Dr. Adair discovered that Fort Mackinac was generally a very healthy garrison. Accordingly, he focused much of his attention on addressing sanitary conditions, including improving ventilation in the sleeping quarters, fixing stovepipes that leaked coal smoke, and monitoring the cleanliness of the water in the well behind the soldiers' barracks.

Mackinac State Historic Parks

Joseph Leggett, ca. 1879 from the *Mackinac Island News*, August 20, 1938

Sergeant Joseph M. Leggett

1853–1938

Joseph Leggett joined the army in 1875 and served the final 18 months of his five-year enlistment at Fort Mackinac. He was promoted twice at Fort Mackinac and was honorably discharged as a company sergeant. Shortly before leaving the army, Leggett married Mary Amanda Chapman, daughter of John Chapman and granddaughter of former probate court judge and village president Bela Chapman. After leaving the army, Leggett remained at Mackinac and worked variously as a laborer, house painter, and fish market operator. Leggett was also involved in the carriage business and signed the 1898 petition that led to the village ordinance banning automobiles.

James V. Evans

George Gardner McVey

Musician George Gardner McVey

1853–1917

George G. McVey served two separate enlistments in the U.S. Army. During his first term (1870–1875), McVey was a trumpeter assigned to the 8th U.S. Cavalry and served in the 1874–1875 campaign against the Kiowa, Comanche, and Cheyenne Indians in the Southwest. McVey reenlisted in 1878 and served as a musician with Company C, 10th Infantry, at Fort Mackinac from May 1879 to his discharge four years later. In June 1883, he married Mackinac Island resident Harriet Abigail (Abbie) Ranville. The McVeys eventually moved to Mackinaw City and helped operate the Mackinaw City House hotel with Abbie's parents. McVey's great-grandson, James V. Evans, has worked as tour guide at Colonial Michilimackinac (Mackinaw City) interpreting Straits of Mackinac area military history for over 40 years.

Mackinac State Historic Parks

Fort Mackinac Military Band, ca. 1880, at the corner of Mackinac Island's Astor and Main Streets

Fort Mackinac Military Band

At smaller posts like Fort Mackinac, military musicians (drummers, buglers, and fifers) were sometimes joined by other brass and percussion instruments to form small garrison bands. Typically, these bands played at festive and patriotic occasions in the village or fort. On May 30, 1885, the Fort Mackinac Military Band led a long and impressive procession of soldiers, veterans, clergy, and civilians from the village to the post cemetery during Mackinac Island's Decoration Day observance.

Dr. William H. Corbusier, ca. 1895

Dr. William H. Corbusier

1844–1930

Born in New York City, William Corbusier joined the Illinois volunteers as an acting assistant surgeon in 1864 during the Civil War. Following the war, Corbusier returned to New York and completed his medical studies at Bellevue Medical Hospital College. He rejoined the army as a contract surgeon until he was appointed to the army medical corps in 1876. Reflecting on his service at Fort Mackinac in 1882–1884, Dr. Corbusier wrote, "We enjoyed the society of many of the people who spent the summer here and had picnics, dances, drives, sails in sail boats and on the fine yachts fishing and berry parties. In winter we had skating and coasting." Corbusier lived with his wife, Fanny, and five sons in the west apartment of the officers' quarters adjacent to the commanding officer's house.

Major George Keyports Brady, ca. 1888

Pennsylvania State Archives, MG-249.1 Brady Family Papers

Captain George Keyports Brady

1839–1899

George K. Brady's military career began when he enlisted as a private with the Pennsylvania Volunteers at the outbreak of the Civil War. Within a few months he was commissioned as a lieutenant in the regular army and participated in several battles in Virginia and Pennsylvania. Following the war, Brady was transferred to the 23rd Regiment of Infantry and commanded Fort Mackinac in 1884–1886. Like the other commandants after 1875, Brady also served as superintendent of Mackinac National Park and worked to balance military and recreational activities in the park. In 1885, this included curtailing summer target practice in order to avoid "shooting some of the tourists who frequent the island." Brady retired from the army in 1894 and died five years later.

Captain Greenleaf Austin Goodale, ca. 1886

Mackinac State Historic Parks

Captain Greenleaf Austin Goodale

1839–1915

Greenleaf A. Goodale joined the Maine Volunteers as a private at the beginning of the Civil War. He was subsequently promoted corporal and sergeant and fought in multiple battles including the Siege of Yorktown, Second Bull Run, and Gettysburg. In 1864 he accepted a commission as a lieutenant with the 77th U.S. Colored Infantry. Goodale was appointed to the 23rd Regiment of Infantry after the war and served at several western posts before being transferred to Fort Mackinac in 1884. Goodale commanded the island post from 1886 to 1890 and instituted several changes designed to improve the lives of his soldiers. This included creating the post canteen in 1889, where soldiers could play billiards, read the latest magazines, and enjoy sandwiches and beer. Goodale also had the parade ground buildings painted brown instead of white in order to reduce the glare on his men's eyes. Goodale retired from the army as a brigadier general in 1915.

Mackinac State Historic Parks, Acc. No. 1955.200.1

Painting of Fort Mackinac, unknown artist, ca. 1890

This painting from ca. 1890 depicts the east end of the village of Mackinac Island, the military garden and associated buildings, and a portion of the south elevation of the fort. The sentry box above the south sally port shows the brown color scheme ordered by Captain Goodale in 1888.

Mackinac State Historic Parks

Mary Hitchcock Cowles

Mackinac State Historic Parks

Calvin D. Cowles Jr., 1886

Mackinac State Historic Parks

David H. Cowles, 1890

United States Military Academy

West Point graduation photograph of Cadet Calvin Duvall Cowles, 1873

Lieutenant Calvin Duvall Cowles

1849–1937

Calvin D. Cowles graduated from West Point in 1873 and spent the first 11 years of his service at western posts in Arizona, Nebraska, Kansas, Oklahoma, and New Mexico. Cowles moved with his wife Mary Ella and four children to Fort Mackinac in July 1884 and was delighted to be serving in this "desirable station." "I like this place first rate," he wrote two days after arriving. "My quarters are good and duties agreeable. I think I can stand four years of it very well." His initial posting to the island fort lasted only two months, but he returned in 1887 and spent two more years at Mackinac. His fondness for Mackinac Island was tempered by the loss of two children, Josiah in 1884 and Isabel in 1888, both buried in the Fort Mackinac post cemetery. Along with his normal garrison responsibilities, Cowles and Lieutenant Benjamin Morse surveyed and staked the lots on the East and West Bluffs in Mackinac National Park in the fall of 1884. The survey made possible the construction of summer cottages the following year.

Mackinac State Historic Parks

Lieutenant Benjamin C. Morse, ca. 1886

Mackinac State Historic Parks

Jessie Cable Morse, ca. 1886

Mackinac State Historic Parks, Acc. No. 1993.9.11

Cadet jacket of Benjamin C. Morse, U.S. Military Academy at West Point, 1880–1884

Lieutenant Benjamin Clark Morse

1859–1933

An 1884 graduate of West Point, Benjamin C. Morse spent his first six years (except for six months at nearby Fort Brady) on active duty at Fort Mackinac. While at the island fort, Morse met Jessie Cable, daughter of James F. Cable, owner of the Astor House. Following her graduation from Wellesley College, Jessie and Benjamin were married on March 6, 1890, at the Astor House and moved into his apartment in the Officers' Stone Quarters. Morse's long military career included garrison duty at western posts, active duty in the Philippines during the Spanish-American War, and command of the 169th Infantry Brigade at Fort Custer, Michigan, during World War I. He retired as a colonel in 1920 after serving his two final years with the Panama Canal Zone Defense Command.

Mackinac State Historic Parks

Lieutenant Benjamin C. Morse overseeing target practice at the Fort Mackinac rifle range, ca. 1886

Mackinac State Historic Parks

Parlor, apartment of Benjamin and Jessie Morse, officers' stone quarters, 1890

Mackinac State Historic Parks

Lieutenant Edward Barton Pratt, ca. 1885

Mackinac State Historic Parks

Mary Louise Pratt

Lieutenant Edward Barton Pratt

1853–1923

Edward Barton Pratt was born in Virginia in 1853, the son of Captain Henry Pratt, who commanded Fort Mackinac in 1858–1861. His maternal grandfather was Captain John Clitz, who commanded the fort from 1834 until his death in 1836. Pratt was commissioned second lieutenant in 1872 and served with the 23rd Regiment of Infantry at Fort Mackinac from 1884 to 1890. Like his father and grandfather before him, Pratt occupied rooms in the Officers' Stone Quarters, where he lived with his wife, Kate, and daughter, Mary Louise. Besides attending to his military responsibilities, Pratt helped organize Fort Mackinac's baseball club and recreational rifle team in 1885. Both clubs competed against teams throughout northern Michigan. Pratt later served in the Philippine-American War in 1898–1901 and was stationed in the Philippines until he retired from the army as a brigadier general in 1909.

Lieutenant Pratt's parlor in the Officers' Stone Quarters, 1887

Fort Mackinac baseball team on the parade ground field north of Fort Mackinac, ca. 1885

Fort Mackinac Rifle Team, 1886. Lieutenant Pratt is standing, third from left; Sergeant George Robinson is standing, far left; First Sergeant Thomas Hennessy is standing, far right.

Mackinac State Historic Parks

Sergeant James B. Martin, Company E, 23rd Infantry, ca. 1884

Mackinac State Historic Parks

Sergeant James B. Martin and Ella Delaney Martin, ca. 1888

Mackinac State Historic Parks, Acc. No. 79.22

James Martin's *Soldier's Handbook*

Sergeant James B. Martin

James B. Martin arrived at Fort Mackinac as a corporal with Company E, 23rd Infantry, in 1884. A farmer by occupation, the Indiana-born Martin was soon promoted to sergeant and lived in the west wing of the second floor of the soldiers' barracks. On July 10, 1888, Martin married Ella A. Delaney, a 23-year-old domestic servant. As a result of two garrison courts-martial, one in August 1888 for being absent without leave from roll call and another in October 1888 for being drunk at afternoon drill, Martin was reduced to the rank of private. He remained at the island fort until the end of his enlistment on March 11, 1891.

Massachusetts Mollus Photograph Collection, U.S. Army Heritage and Education Center, Carlisle, PA

Major William Cheney Manning, 103rd U.S. Colored Troops, ca. 1865

Captain William Cheney Manning

1842–1901

William C. Manning served in the Civil War as a private, musician, corporal, and sergeant major with the Massachusetts Volunteers before accepting a commission as first lieutenant with the 35th U.S. Colored Troops in 1863. Manning saw considerable combat action during the war, was wounded multiple times, and carried a minie ball from the Battle of Bull Run in his hip for the rest of his life. Manning was commissioned in the postwar regular army and appointed to the 23rd Infantry in 1867. He was stationed at posts around the country and fought in the engagement with Apache Indians, at Mazatzal Mountains, Arizona, in December 1872. Manning commanded Company E, 23rd Infantry at Fort Mackinac from 1886 to 1890. His final years were marked by a variety of illnesses, undoubtedly compounded by his multiple battle wounds. Manning died in Washington, DC, at age 59 in 1901 and is buried in Arlington National Cemetery.

Mackinac State Historic Parks

Quartermaster Sergeant John B. Fletcher, ca. 1890

Mackinac State Historic Parks

Sarah Peachey Fletcher, ca. 1890

Mackinac State Historic Parks, Acc. No. 1989.4.17

John Fletcher's sergeant chevrons, ca. 1885–1893

Post Quartermaster Sergeant John B. Fletcher

1845–1930

John B. Fletcher joined the Pennsylvania Volunteer Infantry during the Civil War when he was 17 years old. This was the beginning of a military life that would continue for nearly 30 years. Fletcher was first appointed post quartermaster sergeant in 1884 and served in this capacity at Fort Mackinac from 1885 until his retirement in 1893. While at Mackinac, Fletcher and wife Sarah lived in the sergeants' quarters on the north parade ground behind Fort Mackinac. Three of their four sons were born while they were at Fort Mackinac. Fletcher was consistently praised by his commanding officers and received a glowing letter of support from Fort Mackinac's Lieutenant Joseph Frazier upon his retirement. His experiences and recommendations helped him land the position of civilian depot quartermaster at the Schuylkill Arsenal (Philadelphia), a position he held until 1918.

John and Sarah Fletcher with sons John, Archibald, and Robert in front of his quarters behind Fort Mackinac, 1891

Mackinac State Historic Parks

Mackinac State Historic Parks

Private Amos Wilkie, ca. 1888

Private Amos Wilkie

New York native Amos Wilkie was assigned to Company E, 23rd Infantry, at Fort Mackinac in July 1886. Over the next four years, Private Wilkie divided much of his time between painting fort buildings and running afoul of military law. In the summer of 1888, while painting the clothing storage building, Wilkie left without permission and went to his quarters to get a drink. Three days later he was brought before a garrison court-martial. Although he was exonerated in this case, Wilkie was found guilty by six other garrison courts while serving at Fort Mackinac. Wilkie transferred with the rest of his company to San Antonio, Texas, in May 1890.

Mackinac State Historic Parks

Sergeant William J. Fenley, 1890

Mackinac State Historic Parks

Corporal William J. Fenley and Mary Eva Toohey, ca. 1889

Sergeant William J. Fenley

b. 1861

A native of Wexford County, Ireland, William Fenley joined the U.S. Army in March 1886 and was assigned to Company E, 23rd Infantry, at Fort Mackinac nine months later. Fenley was promoted twice during his stay at Mackinac and left the island with his company as a sergeant in May 1890. One year earlier, Fenley married Mary Eva Toohey, a milliner living in the village, at Ste. Anne's Roman Catholic Church.

Mackinac State Historic Parks

Enlisted soldiers of Company K, 23rd Infantry, in the first-floor bunk room of the soldiers' barracks, Fort Mackinac, ca. 1886

Soldiers in Barracks Bunk Room

A rare, behind-the-scenes interior photograph of off-duty soldiers relaxing in their barracks. The furnishings include the new, composite iron bunks "supplied with one mattress each, stuffed with cotton, size to fit the bunks, 5 inches thick and 2 extra linen covers to each mattress, one cotton pillow each, and two pillow cases and four sheets to each bed." "Such accommodations," continued post surgeon John R. Bailey, "are very much better than those furnished by ordinary hotels and may be said to be truly luxurious. They are conducive to sweet repose, comfort, cleanliness, contentment and health. With all these comfortable surroundings . . . the enlisted men of the U.S. Army ought to be satisfied and should consider themselves far above the average laborer and act accordingly."

Mackinac State Historic Parks

Lieutenant George B. Davis, ca. 1886

Lieutenant George Burwell Davis

1862–1935

New York native George Burwell Davis graduated from West Point in 1886 and was immediately assigned to the 23rd Infantry at Fort Mackinac. During his three years at Mackinac, the young lieutenant received significant training in garrison administration duties. He served, at different times, as signal officer, ordnance officer, post treasurer, quartermaster, and commissary of subsistence. In June 1888 he escorted two prisoners found guilty by general courts-martial to prison at Fort Leavenworth, Kansas. In the 1890s Davis began working in the Army Commissary of Subsistence Department and received several promotions before retiring as a colonel in the Quartermaster's Department in 1916. During World War I, Davis served as inspector of shells at the Milton Manufacturing Company's plant in Milton, Pennsylvania.

Companies E and K, 23rd Infantry, ca. 1886

Mackinac State Historic Parks

Soldiers at the post guardhouse. Notice the water buckets for fire prevention next to the guardhouse and the 10-inch mortar shells stacked in the foreground.

Mackinac State Historic Parks

Soldiers in Prussian-inspired dress uniforms march through the North Sally Port to the large parade ground behind Fort Mackinac. Captain Greenleaf A. Goodale is the officer on the left in the foreground.

Mackinac State Historic Parks

Soldiers in the undress or fatigue uniform assembled in front of the soldiers' barracks.

Mackinac State Historic Parks

Dr. Charles E. Woodruff, ca. 1895

Dr. Charles Edward Woodruff

1860–1915

Charles E. Woodruff attended the U.S. Naval Academy at Annapolis for three and a half years before resigning in protest over the expulsion of another student. Changing careers, Woodruff received his medical degree from Jefferson Medical College, Philadelphia, and was commissioned in the navy on May 17, 1886. Dr. Woodruff transferred to the army one year later and, after briefly serving at Fort Wayne, Detroit, was sent to Fort Mackinac in July 1887. Like all of the fort's surgeons, Woodruff wrestled with the problem of intemperance. In September 1887, he complained of an "epidemic of drunkenness and general deviltry" brought on by "the departure of numerous female employees of the various summer hotels just closed, each departure being mourned by a 'drunk.'" Following his years at Mackinac, Woodruff was stationed in California before serving in the field in Cuba during the Spanish-American War. Dr. Woodruff retired as a lieutenant colonel and medical inspector in 1913.

James Higgens and Greg Hosmer, in Memory of Ruth McVay Hosmer

Captain Harlan Ellsworth McVay

Dr. Harlan Ellsworth McVay

1861–1899

Harlan McVay began his military career as an army contract physician assigned to Fort Mackinac on June 20, 1889. Following an examination before the Army Medical Examining Board in New York, McVay was commissioned first lieutenant and assistant surgeon at Fort Mackinac on October 29, 1889. McVay lived with his wife, Flora, and daughter, Jessie, who was born at the island fort in January 1890. In his spare time, McVay, "with the assistance of Mrs. McVay," compiled a list of 242 Mackinac Island "wild plants and flowers" that he recorded in the "Medical History of the Post" in October 1891. McVay served with troops during the Philippine-American War and died in Manila of typhoid fever on January 4, 1899.

Edwin M. Coates

Major Edwin M. Coates

1836–1913

Edwin M. Coates enlisted in the New York Volunteers at the outbreak of the Civil War but resigned his volunteer commission four months later to enter the regular army as second lieutenant in the 2nd Dragoons. Coates served throughout the war and was injured in a fall from his horse at the Battle of the Wilderness in May 1864. Coates was retained in the post war army and served at several western posts before being assigned to command Fort Mackinac in 1890. Like his predecessors, Coates divided his time between commanding his troops and running the national park. He especially struggled with a budget that was "entirely inadequate" for the maintenance and improvement of the national park and urged the sale of federal property on nearby Bois Blanc Island and using the proceeds for the island park. Coates retired from the service on January 29, 1900, nearly four decades after his initial enlistment.

Massachusetts Mollus Photograph Collection, U.S. Army Heritage and Education Center, Carlisle, PA

Charles T. Witherell, ca. 1863

Mackinac State Historic Parks

Captain Charles T. Witherell, ca. 1890

Captain Charles T. Witherell

1837–1928

Charles T. Witherell's military career began when he joined the Maine Volunteers as a sergeant in May 1861 at the beginning of the Civil War. Within a year Witherell was offered an officer's commission, and he led troops in several engagements throughout the war. He was wounded at the battles of Rappahannock Station and Spotsylvania. Witherell was commissioned into the regular army following the war and served as a company commander at Fort Mackinac from 1890 to 1894. Post commandant Major Clarence Bennett used a March 1894 efficiency report to praise Witherell as a "successful company commander." Bennet added, "He has an excellent company, one of the best evidences of zeal and ability in performance of military duty."

United States Military Academy

Cadet Edmund Dickinson Smith, ca. 1879

Lieutenant Edmund Dickinson Smith

1857–1900

An 1879 graduate of West Point, Edmund D. Smith served at several western posts before returning to the Military Academy as an instructor of mathematics for four years beginning in 1884. During his brief service with Company D, 19th Infantry, at Fort Mackinac (May 1890–May 1891), Smith was responsible for quartermaster and commissary supplies. After Mackinac, Smith returned to teach at West Point before returning to garrison duty in 1895. Smith was still with the 19th Infantry when he died on February 5, 1900, from wounds received in action the previous day during the Philippine-American War.

Special Collections & Archives Department, Nimitz Library, U.S. Naval Academy

Lieutenant Zebulon Baird Vance

1860–1924

Lieutenant Vance was the son of Zebulon Baird Vance Sr., an officer in the Confederacy and governor of North Carolina during the Civil War. Vance Sr. remained in politics after the war and served as U.S. senator and was once again elected governor of North Carolina in 1877. Vance Jr. attended the U.S. Naval Academy but resigned in 1883, joining Charles Woodruff (Fort Mackinac, 1887–1889) and others who protested the expulsion of a fellow student. Vance was commissioned as a second lieutenant in the 19th Infantry in 1884 and was on garrison duty in several posts before serving briefly at Fort Mackinac in 1890. During the Spanish-American War Vance participated in the campaign to occupy Puerto Rico in 1898. Vance retired from the army in 1908 but was recalled to active duty during World War I for duty along the Mexican border. He subsequently commanded Fort Niagara, New York (1917), and was quartermaster general, Atlantic Coastal Defenses, until his second retirement in 1919.

Zebulon Baird Vance, as a midshipman at the U.S. Naval Academy at Annapolis, Maryland, ca. 1880

Cadet Henry Grant Learnard, ca. 1890

United States Military Academy

Lieutenant Henry Grant Learnard

1867–1937

Fort Mackinac was Henry G. Learnard's first duty assignment after graduating from West Point in 1890. During his two-year stay at Mackinac, Lieutenant Learnard cut his teeth on garrison administration by serving variously as ordnance officer, post adjutant, post treasurer, recruiting officer, officer in charge of the post exchange, and temporary commandant of the post in September 1892. Learnard helped lead 60 soldiers from Fort Mackinac to Chicago in October 1892 to participate in the dedication ceremony for the World's Columbian Exposition commemorating the 400th anniversary of Christopher Columbus's voyage to North America in 1492. Learnard had a wide-ranging military career after leaving Mackinac. This included service in the Boxer Rebellion in China, the Philippine-American War, and the Panama Canal Zone. Learnard received the Army Distinguished Service Medal for reorganizing and administering the Adjutant General's Department during World War I. Learnard retired as a brigadier general in 1931 and died six years later.

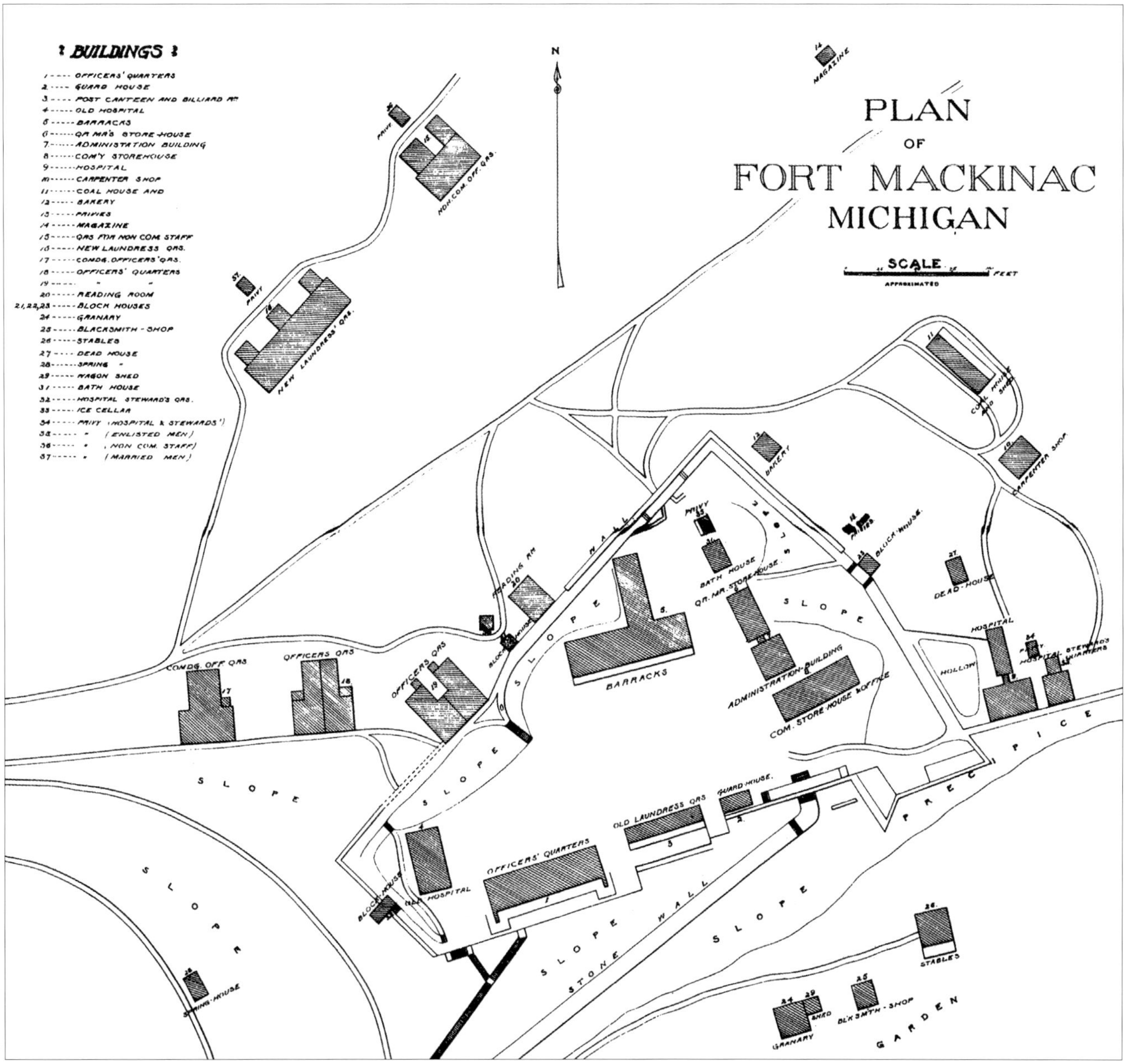

Plan of Fort Mackinac, 1890

This 1890 plan shows the fort as it appeared during the final years of military occupation. A number of buildings, including several residences, were constructed outside the original protective walls in later years as the fort's military importance began to wane.

Private Thomas Frost, Company C, 19th Infantry, 1892

Private Thomas Frost

Thomas Frost served at Fort Mackinac for 13 months in 1890–1891. While at the island fort, the Scottish-born private served on special duty as a company cook and on extra duty as a laborer in the subsistence department. Frost transferred to Company F at Fort Brady on June 8, 1891. The photograph was taken at W. J. Bell's Studio at Sault Ste. Marie on November 16, 1892.

Mackinac State Historic Parks

Private Edward Martin, Company D, 19th Infantry, ca. 1893

Private J. Edward Martin

Private J. Edward Martin joined the army in Logansport, Indiana, on February 26, 1891, and arrived at Fort Mackinac two days later. Martin was promoted to wagoner on April 1, 1892, and transferred, with rest of Company D, to Fort Brady seven months later.

Enlisted men, 19th Infantry, at Foley Photography Studio, Mackinac Island, ca. 1891

Enlisted men from Companies C and D, 19th Infantry, photographed in the Foley Photograph Studio on the corner of Main and Fort Streets. These were the last companies that served Fort Mackinac before it was abandoned in 1895. Prior to the advent of personal cameras in the early 20th century, photographs were taken by professionals. Foley's studio boasted several hand-painted backdrop scenes, including the island's famous Arch Rock. These photographs were mounted on cabinet cards featuring decorative borders and the name of the studio.

Mackinac State Historic Parks

Mackinac State Historic Parks

Mackinac State Historic Parks

Mackinac State Historic Parks

Mackinac State Historic Parks

Mackinac State Historic Parks

Mackinac State Historic Parks

Mackinac State Historic Parks

Mackinac State Historic Parks

Courtesy U.S. National Library of Medicine

Dr. Edwin F. Gardner

Dr. Edwin F. Gardner

1848–1930

Born in Charlotte, Maine, Edwin Gardner was just 16 years old when he was "seized with an insane desire to be a soldier" and joined the Maine Volunteers in 1865 just as the Civil War was coming to a close. Following the war, Gardner returned to his studies and graduated from Harvard Medical School in 1875. He was commissioned into the U.S. Army Medical Corps the following year and served as Fort Mackinac's last regular army doctor from 1892 to 1894. In a June 1893 description of the post, Dr. Gardner proudly reported that the "food of the troops is good in quality and sufficient quantity." In addition to the army ration, Gardner noted that the soldiers enjoyed the "products of the post garden . . . in which are raised potatoes, beets, onions, green corn, cabbage, lettuce, cucumbers, carrots, parsnips, etc. . . . and cows furnishing milk sufficient for the coffee and cooking purposes."

Roger Hunt Collection, U.S. Army Heritage and Education Center, Carlisle, PA

Lieutenant Colonel Clarence E. Bennett, 1st California Volunteer Cavalry, ca. 1864

Major Clarence Edmund Bennett

1833–1902

An 1855 graduate of West Point, Clarence Bennett served for only five years before resigning his commission in 1860. Bennett returned to military life as a major in the 1st California Volunteer Cavalry in 1863. He was reappointed to the regular army after the war and served at several western posts before being assigned to Fort Mackinac. During his eight months at Mackinac, Bennett commanded the last full company of soldiers at the island fort as the post was reduced to a single lieutenant and 11 enlisted men in October 1894, prior to its final closure in September 1895.

Notes

1. Louise Kellogg, *The British Regime in Wisconsin and the Northwest* (Madison: State Historical Society of Wisconsin Press, 1971), 183–185.
2. Brian L. Dunnigan, *King's Men at Mackinac: The British Garrisons, 1780–1796* (Mackinac Island: Mackinac Island State Park Commission, 1973), 22.
3. Anthony Wayne to Henry Burbeck, August 17, 1796, *Fort Mackinac Orderly Book, 1796–1799*, West Point Museum (West Point), transcript copy, Mackinac Island State Park Commission, Petersen Center, Mackinaw City.
4. James Wilkinson to Henry Burbeck, August 19, 1797, *Fort Mackinac Orderly Book.*
5. Alexander Hamilton to David Strong, May 22, 1799, Papers of Alexander Hamilton, Library of Congress, Washington, DC. Selected letters relating to Mackinac Island copied and in the collection of Mackinac Island State Park Commission, Petersen Center, Mackinaw City.
6. Information about U.S. military officers found in Francis B. Heitman, *Historical Register and Dictionary of the United States Army from Its Organization, September 29, 1789, to March 2, 1903*, 2 vols. (Urbana: University of Illinois Press, 1965).
7. Thomas M. Exley, *A Compendium of the Pay of the Army, from 1785 to 1888* (Washington, DC, 1888), 48–51.
8. Garrison Orders, Michilimackinac, December 1, 1804, and December 2, 1804, Orderly Book of Jacob Kingsbury, 1804–1805, New York Historical Society, New York.
9. Charles Roberts to John Glegg, July 29, 1812, *Select British Documents of the Canadian War of 1812*, ed. William Wood (Toronto: Champlain Society, 1920–1928), 1: 438–441.
10. Richard Bullock to Noah Freer, October 23, 1813, *Michigan Pioneer and Historical Collections*, 15: 424–425.
11. George Prevost to Henry Bathurst, July 10, 1814, *Michigan Pioneer and Historical Collections*, 25:585.
12. George Prevost to Henry Bathurst, March 12, 1814, *Michigan Pioneer and Historical Collections*, 25: 575–576.
13. "Return of November, 1816," Fort Mackinac, Michigan, Post Returns, 1816–1895, Records of the Adjutant General's Office, RG 94, National Archives, Washington, DC.
14. Brian L. Dunnigan, *Fort Holmes* (Lansing: Mackinac Island State Park Commission, 1984).
15. George Graham, Chief Clerk, Department of War to Commanding Officer at Fort Michilimackinac and Wm. H. Puthuff, Indian Agent, June 5, 1816, *Wisconsin Historical Collections*, 19: 414.
16. "Returns of June, 1820, May, 1821 and June, 1821,"

Fort Mackinac, Michigan, Post Returns, 1816–1895, Records of the War Department, Office of the Adjutant General, National Archives, Washington, DC.

17. Entries for June 29 and July 3, 1939, Letter Book of Ordnance Sergeant R. J. Dunn, U.S. Army, 1837–1843, Manuscript copy in Mackinac State Historic Parks Library, Petersen Center, Mackinaw City.
18. "Fort Mackinac Muster Rolls," Company "L," 4th Artillery, October 1856; Company "E," 2nd Artillery, June–August 1857; Company "G," 2nd Artillery, April 1861, Fort Mackinac Muster Rolls, Records of the Adjutant General's Office, RG 94, National Archives, Washington, DC.
19. Heitman, *Historical Register and Dictionary*, vol. 1; Norman Stevens, "Commissioned Officers of the Army of the United States at Fort Mackinac," unpublished manuscript, Mackinac State Historic Parks Library, Petersen Center, Mackinaw City.
20. Exley, *Compendium*, 49.
21. Lt. John Phelps to Elizabeth Tower, July 1, 1840, John W. Phelps Papers, New York Public Library.
22. Exley, *Compendium*, 51.
23. Between 1812 and 1860 nonfarm laborers earned between $22 and $32 per month. Conference on Research in Income and Wealth, "Nineteenth Century Wage Trends," *Trends in the American Economy in the Nineteenth Century* (Princeton, NJ: Princeton University Press, 1960), 462.
24. Edward M. Coffman, *The Old Army: A Portrait of the American Army in Peacetime, 1784–1898* (New York: Oxford University Press, 1986), 141.
25. Andrew Jones, "Company Profile: Company G, Fifth Regiment, U.S. Infantry, 1829," and Phil Porter, "Statistical Analysis, Company 'G,' 2nd Artillery, 1860," unpublished manuscripts, Mackinac State Historic Parks, Petersen Center, Mackinaw City.
26. "Promulgated proceedings of a General Court Martial at Fort Mackinac," October 7, 1851, Private Wolf Grenner, Company "A," 4th Artillery. General Court Martial File HH98, Records of the Office of the Judge Advocate General (Army), RG 153, National Archives, Washington DC.
27. "Inspection Report, Fort Mackinac, July 14, 1826," Selected Inspection Reports, Fort Mackinac, 1824–1890, Records of the Officer of the Inspector General, RG 159, National Archives, Washington, DC.
28. Brian L. Dunnigan, *A Picturesque Situation: Mackinac before Photography, 1615–1860* (Detroit: Wayne State University Press, 2008), 174–178, 299, 322–325.
29. Orders No. 70, Fort Mackinac, September 14, 1844, and Orders No. 85, Fort Mackinac, November 14, 1844. Volume 32, Orders, September 4, 1844–September 17, 1860, Records of the United States Army Continental Commands (Army Posts), Fort Mackinac, Michigan, RG 393, National Archives, Washington, DC.
30. General Courts Martial of Charles Benedict and William Henderson, September 3, 1860, Records of the Judge Advocate General, RG 153, National Archives, Washington, DC.
31. General Courts Martial of Charles Eddo, E. V. Francis, James Shearer, Christopher Genury, Henry Gretzler, Hugh Urquardt, Peter White, and Whitman Taylor, May 13, 1830, Records of the Judge Advocate General, RG 153, National Archives, Washington, DC.
32. Lt. Colonel Enos Cutler to Acting Assistant Adjutant General, Department Headquarters, New York, September 6, 1820; Fort Mackinac, Letters Sent, 1829–1836, Records of the United States Army Continental Commands, RG 393, National Archives, Washington DC
33. General Court Martial of Ephraim Kirby Smith, August 9, 1830, Records of the Judge Advocate General, RG 153, National Archives, Washington, DC.
34. Norman Stevens, "An Interesting Interlude: The Detention of Confederate Political Prisoners at Fort Mackinac, Michigan in the Summer of 1862," unpublished manuscript, Mackinac State Historic Parks, Petersen Center, Mackinaw City, n.d., 7–8.
35. Stevens, "An Interesting Interlude," 9–25; Richard Shaul, "Rebel Resort, Imprisoned at Fort Mackinac," *Michigan History Magazine*, July–August (1998): 28–33.

36. Maurice Matloff, general editor, *Army Historical Series, American Military History* (Washington, DC: Office of the Chief of Military History, United States Army, 1969), 282.
37. "Returns of June, 1866–May, 1869," Fort Mackinac, Michigan, Post Returns, 1816–1895, Records of the Adjutant General's Office, RG 94, National Archives, Washington, DC.
38. Keith Widder, *Mackinac National Park, 1875–1895*, Reports in Mackinac History and Archaeology, no. 4 (Mackinac Island: Mackinac Island State Park Commission, 1975), 8–27.
39. Correspondence of the Fort Mackinac Quartermaster, 1874–1877, Records of the Quartermaster General, RG 92, National Archives, Washington, DC; Mackinac Island State Park Commission, "Historic Structures Report, Sergeant's Quarters, Fort Mackinac," September 5–7, 9–10, 1994.
40. Mackinac Island State Park Commission, "Historic Structures Report, Soldiers Barracks, Fort Mackinac," September 11–12, 1994.
41. "Report of the General of the Army," Headquarters Army of the United States, Washington, DC, October 27, 1883; *Annual Report of the Secretary of War for the Year 1883* (Washington, DC: Government Printing House, 1883), 1: 47.
42. Jack D. Foner, *The United States Soldier between Two Wars: Army Life and Reforms, 1865–1898* (New York: Humanities Press, 1970), 77–79; William Manning to Adjutant General, December 31, 1889, vol. 18, May 4, 1889–January 30, 1891, Fort Mackinac, Letters Sent, 1829–1836, Records of the United States Army Continental Commands, RG 393, National Archives, Washington DC; Telegram from Captain Greenleaf A. Goodale to Assistant Adjutant General, Governors Island, NY, December 20, 1889, Fort Mackinac "Telegrams Sent," vol. 25a, November 6, 1888–November 30, 1894. Records of the United States Army Continental Commands, RG 393, National Archives, Washington, DC.
43. Journal Entry, Dr. John R. Bailey, May 13, 1885, "Medical History, Fort Mackinac, Michigan 1871–1877," pp. 13–30, Records of the Adjutant General's Office, RG 94, National Archives, Washington, DC.
44. Journal Entries, Dr. John R. Bailey, November 30, 1885, and December 31, 1885, "Medical History, Fort Mackinac, Michigan 1871–1877," pp. 13–30, Records of the Adjutant General's Office, RG 94, National Archives, Washington, DC.
45. Order No. 118, October 8, 1889, Records of the United States Army Continental Commands (Army Posts), Fort Mackinac, Michigan, RG 393, National Archives, Washington, DC.
46. Telegrams from Lt. George Davis to Lieutenant Lea Febiger, Sault Ste. Marie, Michigan, March 17, March 18, March 19, March 21, 1889, Fort Mackinac "Telegrams Sent," vol. 25a, November 6, 1888–November 30, 1894, Records of the United States Army Continental Commands, RG 393, National Archives, Washington, DC.
47. "Fund of the Fort Mackinac Base Ball Club," Roster 1885 and 1890–1893, Records of the Adjutant General's Office, RG 94, National Archives, Washington, DC.
48. Don Rickey, *Forty Miles a Day on Beans and Hay: The Enlisted Soldier Fighting the Indian Wars* (Norman: University of Oklahoma Press, 1963), 126–127.
49. Coffman, *Old Army*, 346.
50. Coffman, *Old Army*, 346; Foner, *United States Soldier*, 16.
51. Leslie Smith to Assistant Adjutant General, Headquarters, Department of the Lakes, July 1, 1872, Fort Mackinac, Letters Sent, 1829–1836, Records of the United States Army Continental Commands, RG 393, National Archives, Washington DC.
52. Order No. 12, February 27, 1886, Records of the United States Army Continental Commands (Army Posts), Fort Mackinac, Michigan, RG 393, National Archives, Washington DC .
53. General Court Martial of Thomas Conroy, May 29, 1888, Records of the Judge Advocate General, RG 153, National Archives, Washington, DC.
54. General Court Martial of Frank Darlington, May 29, 1888, Records of the Judge Advocate General, RG 153,

National Archives, Washington, DC.

55. General Court Martial of Frank Darlington, November 23, 1888, Records of the Judge Advocate General, RG 153, National Archives, Washington, DC.

56. "Register of Enlistments, 1867–1897," reels 33–48, "United States Register of Enlistments," microfilm copy number 233, National Archives, Washington, DC.

57. "Register of Enlistments, 1867–1897."

58. Heitman, *Historical Register and Dictionary*, vol. 1; Stevens, "Commissioned Officers ."

59. Exley, *Compendium*, 49.

60. Stevens, "William Notson," "William H. Corbusier," and "Edwin F. Gardner," in "Commissioned Officers."

61. Stevens, "John R. Bailey," in "Commissioned Officers"; John R. Bailey, M.D., *Mackinac, Formerly Michilimackinac, History and Guidebook* (Grand Rapids: Tradesman Company, 1909), 9–11; William Manning to Assistant Adjutant General, April 20, 1889, Fort Mackinac, Letters Sent, 1829–1836, Records of the United States Army Continental Commands, RG 393, National Archives, Washington DC.

62. Foner, *United States Soldier*, 2.

Bibliographical Essay

Multiple primary and secondary sources were consulted in preparing the introductory essay and captions. Copies of most of these documents and books are in the Mackinac State Historic Parks Petersen Center Library, Mackinaw City, Michigan. This library, which is a repository for items focused on the long and rich history of the Straits of Mackinac, was started under the leadership of Dr. Eugene T. Petersen and substantially expanded through the efforts of Dr. David A. Armour, Dr. Keith R. Widder, Phil Porter, Steven C. Brisson, and Brian Jaeschke.

U.S. military records, comprised mainly of reports filed by Fort Mackinac officers, provide a vast array of information about Fort Mackinac. The majority of these documents are held by the National Archives and Records Administration in Washington, DC. This includes Inspection Reports from the Records of the Office of the Inspector General, RG 159; Consolidated Correspondence File on Fort Mackinac, Michigan, 1819–1890, Records of the Office of the Quartermaster General, RG 92; Medical History of Fort Mackinac in three volumes (1871–1877, 1878–1887, 1888–1893), Fort Mackinac Muster Rolls, 1796–1895, and Summary Court Records, 1890–1894, Records of the Adjutant General's Office, RG 94; Orderly Books 1844–1894, Records of United States Army Commands (Army Posts), Fort Mackinac, Michigan, RG 393; General Courts Martial proceedings, 1829–1890, Records of the Judge Advocate General, RG 153.

Other primary sources used include Henry Burbeck Papers, United States Military Academy Library, Special Collections Division, West Point, New York; Samuel Peter Heintzelman Papers, 1822–1913, and Papers of Alexander Hamilton, Library of Congress (Washington, DC); Orderly Book of Jacob Kingsbury, 1804–1805, The New-York Historical Society (New York); John McNeil Orderly Books, 1813–1825, New Hampshire Historical Society (Concord); John Wolcott Phelps Papers, New York Public Library (New York); Moses Porter Papers and Benjamin K. Pierce Papers, Burton Historical Collection, Detroit Public Library; William Chapman File, Neville Public Museum (Green Bay, WI); Pemberton Family Papers, Historical Society of Pennsylvania (Philadelphia); C. J. Cowles Papers, Southern Historical Collection, University of North Carolina (Chapel Hill); Letter Book, business correspondence of Mackinac Island merchants Alexander Toll (July 1852) and Bromilow and Bates, 1869–1874, and *Letter Book of Ordnance Sergeant R. J. Dunn, U.S. Army, 1837–1843,* Mackinac State Historic Parks' Petersen Center Library, Mackinaw City, Michigan; Smith, Ephraim Kirby, biographical file, Onondaga Historical Association Research Center (Syracuse, NY).

Norman Stevens, unpublished research report, "Commissioned Officers of the Army of the United States at Fort Mackinac" [1997], and Francis B. Heitman's *Historical Register and Dictionary of the United States Army from Its Organization, September 29, 1789, to March 2, 1903* (Washington, DC: Government Printing Office, 1903) were especially helpful in providing biographical information about Fort Mackinac officers.

Printed primary sources include *Michigan Pioneer and Historical Collections,* vols. 10, 15, and 25 (Lansing: Michigan Historical Commission, 1886, 1890, and 1894); *Wisconsin Historical Collections*, vol. 19 (Madison: State Historical Society of Wisconsin, 1910); and Robert Wooster, ed., *Soldier, Surgeon, Scholar: The Memoirs of William Henry Corbusier, 1844–1930* (Norman: University of Oklahoma Press, 2003).

A number of secondary sources were consulted in this project, including Brian L. Dunnigan, *A Picturesque Situation: Mackinac before Photography, 1615–1860* (Detroit: Wayne State University Press, 2008); Edward Coffman, *The Old Army: A Portrait of the American Army in Peacetime, 1784–1898* (New York: Oxford University Press, 1986); Louise Kellogg, *The British Regime in Wisconsin and the Northwest* (Madison: State Historical Society of Wisconsin, 1935); Maurice Matloff, general editor, *Army Historical Series, American Military History* (Washington, DC: Office of the Chief of Military History, United States Army, 1969); Don Rickey, *Forty Miles a Day on Beans and Hay: The Enlisted Soldier Fighting the Indian War* (Norman: University of Oklahoma Press, 1963); Jack D. Foner, *The United States Soldier between Two Wars: Army Life and Reforms, 1865–1898* (New York: Humanities Press, 1970); Colonel Landman, *Adventures and Recollection* (London: Colburn and Co., 1852); Dwight H. Kelton, *Annals of Fort Mackinac* (Chicago: Fergus Printing, 1882).

Since 1960, the Mackinac Island State Park Commission has shared the history of the Straits of Mackinac with the public through its extensive publication program. Over 100 titles have been published by Mackinac State Historic Parks. The following publications were consulted in this work.

Armour, David A., and Keith R. Widder. *At the Crossroads: Michilimackinac during the American Revolution.* Mackinac Island: Mackinac Island State Park Commission, 1978.

Dunnigan, Brian L. *The British Army at Mackinac, 1812–1815.* Mackinac Island: Mackinac Island State Park Commission, 1980.

———. *Fort Holmes.* Mackinac Island: Mackinac Island State Park Commission, 1984.

———. *King's Men at Mackinac: The British Garrisons, 1780–1796.* Mackinac Island: Mackinac Island State Park Commission, 1973.

May, George S. *War of 1812: The United States and Great Britain at Mackinac, 1812–1815.* Mackinac Island: Mackinac Island State Park Commission, 1962.

Nicholas, Edward. *Chaplain's Lady: Life and Love at Fort Mackinac.* Mackinac Island: Mackinac Island State Park Commission, 1987.

Petersen, Eugene T. *Mackinac Island: Its History in Pictures.* Mackinac Island: Mackinac Island State Park Commission, 1973.

Porter, Phil, ed. *A Boy at Fort Mackinac: The Diary of Harold Dunbar Corbusier, 1883–1884, 1892.* Mackinac Island: Mackinac Island State Park Commission, 1994.

———. *A Desirable Station: Soldier Life at Fort Mackinac, 1867–1895.* Mackinac Island: Mackinac Island State Park Commission, 2003.

———. *The Eagle at Mackinac: The Establishment of United States Military and Civil Authority on Mackinac Island, 1796–1802.* Mackinac Island: Mackinac Island State Park Commission, 1991.

———. *Mackinac: An Island Famous in These Regions.* Mackinac Island: Mackinac Island State Park Commission, 1998.

Widder, Keith R. *Mackinac National Park, 1875–1895.* Mackinac Island: Mackinac Island State Park Commission, 1975.

———. *Reveille Till Taps: Soldier Life at Fort Mackinac, 1780–1895.* Mackinac Island: Mackinac Island State Park Commission, 1972.

———. *William Beaumont: The Mackinac Years.*

Mackinac Island: Mackinac Island State Park Commission, 1975.

Wilson, Craig. *The Changing Face of Fort Mackinac.* Mackinac Island: Mackinac Island State Park Commission, 2016.

———. *What is Gained but Mackinac? The Battle of Mackinac Island.* Mackinac Island: Mackinac Island State Park Commission, 2014.

Index